The Battle of
BOSWORTH
❀ FIELD ❀

William Hutton, the author, at the age of about eighty years. Bennett's Hill, his home, is in the background. (Engraving from The Life of William Hutton *by Llewellynn Jewitt, 1872)*

The Battle of
BOSWORTH
FIELD

William Hutton

TEMPUS

First published 1788
Second Edition, with additions 1813
Facsimile Reprint (Alan Sutton) 1974
Reprinted in modern type 1999

Introduction © Peter Hammond 1999

Published by:
Tempus Publishing Limited
The Mill, Brimscombe Port
Stroud, Gloucestershire, GL5 2QG

Typesetting and origination by Tempus Publishing Ltd.
Printed and bound in Great Britain.

British Library Cataloguing in Publication Data.
A catalogue record for this book is available from the British
Library.

ISBN 0 7524 1821 1

*Cover illustration: Battle of Bosworth Field. Frieze in Stowe School,
Buckinghamshire. (Photograph courtesy of Geoffrey Wheeler)*

CONTENTS

LIST OF ILLUSTRATIONS

Publisher's Note

The text of the 1813 edition of Hutton's book has been reset in modern type but has been subjected to no significant editorial intervention. Thus all the original grammar, spelling, abbreviations and style are retained. A list of errata included with the 1813 edition have been corrected in the text and a small number of other, obviously typographical, errors noted during preparation have also been amended. Resetting the text has inevitably changed the original page numbering and so where cross-references are made in the text these have been altered to match the new numbering.

INTRODUCTION
William Hutton and the First Edition

William Hutton, the author of *The Battle of Bosworth Field*, is one of a select group of eighteenth-century antiquaries, the historians of the time, whose works are still valuable at the present day. Unlike some of the others, Horace Walpole and John Nichols for example, Hutton was not highly educated and came from very modest merchant stock. He worked all his long life, became very prosperous and was very much a self-made man, a fact which gave him a great deal of satisfaction, although he seems also to have been modest. He was a natural writer and this combined with a clear and sensible judgement makes his works very readable as well as useful.

He was born in Full Street, Derby, on 30 September 1723. His father was a woolcomber and his ancestors had all been traders. His education, such as it was, was very brief. He attended a school in Derby for less than two years from 1728, and in 1730, at the age of seven, he was apprenticed in a silk mill. He had to start at 5 o'clock in the morning and was so small that he had to stand on pattens to reach the the machines: his height when fully grown was only 5ft 6ins. In 1735, during his seven years' apprenticeship, he was one of those chosen to work on silk from the colony of Georgia, for a gown and petticoat for Queen Caroline.

When this apprenticeship – which he claims he never enjoyed or profited from – was over, he was taken on for a second one by his uncle, who was a silk stockinger in Nottingham. His second apprenticeship expired in 1745 and he worked briefly as a journeyman for his uncle until he died in 1746. He had not been happy with his uncle and aunt and he hated the work (he ran away once for a week). While still an apprentice, as Hutton describes it, an 'inclination for books began to expand' and he also began to be interested in book binding. After the death of his uncle Hutton went to live with his sister Caroline, still in Nottingham. He continued to support himself as a stockinger, his sister lent him the £10 cost of the frame, and he persevered as a bookbinder, which trade he had taught himself. To obtain more materials, the cost of which he borrowed from his sister, he walked to London in April 1749, taking three days, spent three days there and walked back. At this stage he decided to open a shop. His eventual aim was a shop in Birmingham but he thought first to try a smaller place until he was better prepared. Thus at Michaelmas 1749 he opened a small bookshop, stationer and bookbinder in Southwell, Nottinghamshire.

Every day he walked there in the morning to open the shop, leaving at 5 o'clock in the morning, frequently carrying heavy stock, and every evening at 4 o'clock he walked back, taking five hours each way to cover the fourteen miles. He accomplished this each day on bread and cheese and half a pint of ale. Rather less than a year later, on 25 May 1750, he moved his bookshop to Birmingham. Virtually all of his stock was the 'refuse' of the library of Ambrose Rudsdell, a Presbyterian minister to whom Hutton's sister Caroline had been a servant and who offered to sell them to Hutton at the latter's own valuation. Hutton having no money he took the two hundredweight of books for £1 7s, signing a note for that amount. His shop in Birmingham was an immediate success, even though there were already three booksellers there, and one year later he moved to a larger shop in the High Street. Here in 1851 he opened the first circulating library in Birmingham which increased his business considerably. In his spare time he also began to write, at this time chiefly poetry.

A few years later, in 1753, his friend and neighbour Mr Grace took in his niece Sarah Cock to act as his housekeeper and about eighteen months later, after what seems to have been a very low-key courtship, Hutton and Miss Cock married. They lived very happily together for forty-one years until she died in 1796. In 1756 he went into the paper trade, opening what was apparently the first paper warehouse in Birmingham. This business was very successful but a paper mill which he had built in 1759 was less successful and he closed it in 1762, losing about £1,000 as a result. Characteristically, he set to work even harder to make up the loss. This failure did not dampen his business activities, though, and in 1766 he began to speculate in the purchase of farms and other land. This he continued to do during the rest of his life, usually with profit but sometimes not. He occasionally ran himself into debt and took the money to pay his creditors from his paper business. He then simply resolved to work even harder and a few years later would record the amount of profit he had made. On one of his plots of land, at Bennett's Hill, Saltley, Warwickshire, he built himself a country house in 1769. This he enlarged at intervals to accommodate his family. In 1772 he bought an old house in High Street, Birmingham. This house was apparently built in 1567, partly of stones from the dissolved priory. Due to an act passed to light and widen the

John Nichols, printer and publisher, at the age of sixty-eight. In 1813, he published the second edition of Hutton's book, which also contained his own additional notes and is the edition from which the present version is taken. (Engraving from Literary Anecdotes of the Eighteenth Century *by William Boyer and John Nichols, 1812, courtesy of of the Thomas Layton Museum Trust)*

streets of Birmingam (and which Hutton rather selfishly, if naturally, opposed), he had to demolish it in 1775. To avoid part of the cost Hutton supervised and took part in the rebuilding himself, the house then fronting on New Street.

During this period, and despite all his hard work, he continued his writing and in 1782 his first book, a *History of Birmingham*, was published in an edition of under 400 copies from which he made a profit of £40. This *History* was of nearly 300 pages, and contained seventeen plates, some of them the only drawings now extant of lost buildings. It was commended by fellow antiquarians and afterwards went through four editions in Hutton's lifetime. It is still of value. Later in 1782 he was elected a Fellow of the Antiquarian Society of Scotland, to his great pride. He remarked that he had not known he was an antiquarian until informed by readers of his *History*.

During this time while working for his living he was also taking part in public affairs, although not in politics. He carefully recorded that he was appointed to his first office on 8 April 1768 as Overseer of the Poor. This pleased him a great deal since, as he said, he thought himself 'beyond my ancestors; for none, within the reach of tradition, had equalled it. They had rather been the poor than overseers of the poor'. In 1772, he became one of the commissioners of the Court of Requests, a tribunal for the recovery of small debts and remained a commissioner for nineteen years. He was president of the Court in 1787. As a result of this he investigated the origin and nature of the Court and of other local courts and published the result of his researches as *The Court of Requests* in 1787. He later published a kind of addendum entitled *A Dissertation on Juries*.

In his spare time Hutton took his family on brief holidays around Birmingham to nearby beauty spots, such as Aston on Trent, where his wife's family had come from, and on one memorable occasion, in 1785, to Buxton. In this same year he published an account of a visit to London in the previous year to attend a trial. As he said, his visit this time was in considerably greater state than his previous one. In 1788 his holiday was to Blackpool, where he notes that he found 'much company, much pride, much vulgarity, accompanied with much good humour.' He was so taken by the place that while there he wrote a short history, since (as he says in the Introduction) he had not been able to find out anything about it and he thought that others might find themselves in the same situation. This pamphlet was reprinted several times. In this same year he published his history of Bosworth, of which more below.

His firm adminstration of justice in the Court of Requests had not endeared him to a part of the population and he received a check in his steadily increasing prosperity and a great shock to his peace of mind in 1791, when riots occurred in Birmingham. These were ostensibly caused by a dinner at Dadley's Hotel in Birmingham to commemorate the outbreak of the French Revolution. Tension was high in the country generally as a result of the Revolution and the authorities were worried that something similar might happen in Britain. The dinner and some inflammatory handbills which were found at the same time seem to have been the sparks which caused the situation to catch fire in Birmingham. The riots were in effect largely directed against Dissenters, (partly because they were thought to be particularly favourable to the Revolution), including Dr Joseph Priestley, the most well known. Hutton was undoubtedly a Dissenter and was known as friend of Priestley although neither Hutton nor Priestley had been present at the dinner. Hutton's house in the High Street was sacked and the one at Bennett's Hill was burned to the ground. Hutton himself was seized by the mob and only escaped personal harm by buying for them 329 gallons of ale. The town magistrates seem to have done little to quell the rioters and they were not stopped until soldiers were sent from London. In his houseless state after the riots he was offered a home by no less than seventeen of his friends, sixteen of them (to his satisfaction) being supporters of the established church. He afterwards (in September 1793) received compensation from the government of £5,390 17s although he reckoned his losses at £8,243 3s 2d. A few months after the riots, in August 1791, he wrote what was in the circumstances a remarkably moderate account of the events which was afterwards published by his daughter. His chief feeling of grievance seems to have been that he had felt he was a valued citizen of Birmingham and that the activities of the mob had let him down. His wife's health had suffered as a result of these experiences and she never really recovered. To his lasting sorrow she died in 1796.

In 1793 during the rebuilding of his house at Bennett's Hill, he suffered an injury to his leg, and this and his losses in the riots seem to have depressed his spirits to the extent that he used the occasion of his son's marriage in 1793 to hand over his business to him. He continued his successful dealings in land, his writing, including poetry which he resumed after a lapse of many years, and after the death of his wife he travelled a great deal in the company of his daughter. They

Chimney Piece in the Great Parlour of the Tankard Alehouse, Ipswich.

The carved chimney piece from an alehouse in Ipswich described by Nichols on page 20. (From The Gentleman's Magazine, *November 1796)*

travelled to many different parts of the country, particularly to Wales and the North, with Hutton walking amazing distances for a man of seventy and beyond. His memoirs take a more consciously 'antiquarian' tone at this time, although they are still interspersed with his typical discursive comments on the people he met and his thoughts on various sights. This tone is more prominent in the books he wrote after the riots than it was before, although it is present in his history of his home town, the *History of Derby*. This was one of his major works, published in 1791 just before the riots.

In 1801 he undertook an expedition remarkable even for him. He had apparently long wished to see Hadrian's Wall and arrangements to do so had at last been made. His daughter went with him part of the way, travelling by pillion, and Hutton walked, all the way. On the way there they went via Lichfield, Liverpool and Penrith, where his daughter left him to go to see the Lakes, and Hutton walked on to Carlisle, then to Bowness-on-Solway, back along the Wall to Newcastle and Wallsend and then all the way back, which took him, he said, seven days and six hours. He then went south to Penrith, Kendal, Preston and Wigan, returning to Birmingham thirty-five days after they had set out. Hutton had walked 601 miles at the age of seventy-eight. The resulting book is most amusing in the descriptions of his meetings with the inhabitants of the countryside alongside the Wall and gives a graphic picture of a desolate but generally hospitable part of the country.

Before age forced him to stop he made other expeditions, although none of them quite so arduous. He made several visits to Scarborough for the sake of his daughter's health and in the ensuing book describes each place they passed through on the way. His comments on all of them, particularly on the larger ones such as York, are valuable as a picture of these towns at the beginning of the nineteenth century before industrialization changed some of them totally. The last book published in his lifetime was an account of a visit to Coatham (on the north Yorkshire coast). As before, it is a very readable account of his visit and of the other places he saw.

After this his health declined slowly. Until the age of eighty-two he says he had considered himself a young man but by the time he was eighty-eight in 1811 he admitted that he 'felt a sensible decay'. Nevertheless he could still walk twelve miles 'with ease' in that year. It was not until he was ninety years of age, in 1813, that he walked into Birmingham from Bennett's Hill for the last time, a distance of two miles. This time he was unable to walk back. He died in his ninety-second year on 20 September 1815.

Note on sources: There has been no full-length biography of William Hutton but there is perhaps no real need for one since we have his own autobiography, together with his history of his family. These were edited several times by his daughter and lastly by Llewellynn Jewitt in 1872 as *The Life of William Hutton and the History of the Hutton Family*. To this edition were added other notes on the family and on Hutton himself. Hutton's own works (which included several volumes of poems, not mentioned above) add a considerable amount of information on his life and his opinions and are all well worth reading.

The Battle of Bosworth Field

This book was Hutton's fourth. It was the fruit of much reading in the sources, which he lists at the end of the Preface, on page 30. His conclusions as to events in the battle, on historic events and on the character of Richard III do not always slavishly follow his sources but show that he has thought about what they say. He was undoubtedly influenced by Walpole's *Historic Doubts* but does not always follow Walpole's opinion.

The first edition of the book was slighter than the present volume. It began with an eight-page Preface, in accordance with Hutton's adopted precept, stated in his *Tour to Scarborough*, 'that, if an author

A carved frieze depicting the Battle of Bosworth Field now in Stowe School, Buckinghamshire, and described by Hutton on p. 19.

wished his book to succeed, he should never send it into the world without a Preface, for the Preface was often the only thing in a book which was read'. Hutton's prefaces are always worth reading. This one includes his amusing observations on antiquities and antiquarians. The Preface was followed by the Introduction comprising a life of Richard III followed by the account of the Battle of Bosworth: in all, some 264 pages, with the frontispiece of Richard III and a map of the battlefield on pages 54 & 55. It was printed in Birmingham in 1788. Hutton went to Bosworth several times when working on his book and his work is valuable in preserving traditions still extant in the eighteenth century and for his observations on the state of the battlefield then. Later, in 1802, he advanced his interest in Richard III to the extent of visiting Richard's birthplace at Fotheringhay. His observations on the state of

Richard is the recumbent figure with the crown, below the horse in the centre. (Photograph courtesy of Geoffrey Wheeler)

the castle at that time are interesting too, since it appears that the removal of the walls for building material had left trenches enabling the visitor to see where the major ground-floor rooms had been.

The second edition was published by John Nichols, who had published Hutton's *History of the Roman Wall*, and to whom Hutton had dedicated that book. Nichols had presumably seen *Bosworth Field* when it was first published and would have been interested in it because of his own work on the history of Leicestershire; he seems to have initiated the second edition himself. His additions, including further observations on the battlefield by Hutton, Nichols and Parr as well as the transcripts of manuscripts and other pictures taken from Nichols' *History of Leicestershire*, add considerably to the value of the book.

KING RICHARD
the III.

From Walpole's Historic Doubts.

THE

BATTLE

OF

BOSWORTH FIELD,

BETWEEN

RICHARD THE THIRD

AND

HENRY EARL OF RICHMOND,

AUGUST 22, 1485.

WHEREIN IS DESCRIBED

THE APPROACH OF BOTH ARMIES,

WITH

PLANS OF THE BATTLE, ITS CONSEQUENCES,
THE FALL, TREATMENT, AND CHARACTER OF RICHARD.

TO WHICH IS PREFIXED, BY WAY OF INTRODUCTION,

A HISTORY OF HIS LIFE TILL HE ASSUMED THE
REGAL POWER.

BY **W. HUTTON**, F.A.S.S.

———

THE SECOND EDITION, WITH ADDITIONS,

BY J. NICHOLS, F.S.A.

LONDON:

PRINTED BY AND FOR NICHOLS, SON, AND BENTLEY,
RED LION PASSAGE, FLEET STREET.

1813.

ADVERTISEMENT

Having requested Mr. Hutton's permission to re-publish his interesting Account of the Battle of Bosworth Field, illustrated by some Engravings from the "History of Leicestershire;" and having asked whether he had any additions to make; my venerable Friend, in a very kind Answer, says,

"I paid a visit in July 1807 to Bosworth Field; but found so great an alteration since I saw it in 1788, that I was totally lost. The manor had been inclosed; the fences were grown up; and my prospect impeded. King Richard's Well, which figures in our Histories, was nearly obliterated; the swamp where he fell become firm land; and the rivulet proceeding from it, lost in an under-drain; so that future inspection is cut off. I wished to sleep in the room, at the Three Tuns in Atherstone, that was the last in which Henry the Seventh slept prior to the Battle (see p. 77); but was not permitted."

In a subsequent Letter, he says,

"I have no other remarks to make upon my last visit to Bosworth Field, than those already communicated to you, but am pleased with your Additions to it. I cannot tell by what mistake the wood came to be 4 or 500 acres (see p. 79); nor can I now call to mind what I conjectured it to be; so make it 4 or 5 acres, or any other number you may think more correct.

"The following account of a chimney-piece, at Gosfield Hall in Essex a seat of the Marquis of Buckingham, is copied from the Fifth Volume of 'The Beauties of England and Wales, 1803,' p. 352.

'In the Library is an antient sculptured chimney-piece in stone, deserving notice from its subject and execution. It represents, in bold relief, the memorable Battle of Bosworth Field, between Richard III. and the Earl of Richmond; and contains twenty-four figures on horseback, with the King lying prostrate under his own charger. Most of the personages introduced are known by the armorial bearings on their shields. Amongst others are, the Duke of Norfolk, the Earls of Surrey and Northumberland, Sir Simon Digby, Sir Walter Blount, Sir William Herbert, Lord Stanley, Sir George Stanley, Sir William Brandon, Lord Edward Stafford, Sir Gilbert Talbot, Sir R. Ratcliffe, Sir T. Tyrrell, Edward Lord Lovell, and the Earl of Oxford. At the extremity of the chimney-piece are small statues of Henry VII. and his Queen, exactly resembling those on the monument in Westminster Abbey. The exact date of this sculpture* is uncertain; but it is known to be of considerable antiquity, it having been removed in the year 1687 from Bois Hall, a small house belonging to the Earls of Oxford, one of whom was a partizan of the Earl of Richmond.'

"The whole of this curious chimney-piece, as appears by a newspaper of the year 1808, has been removed, to decorate the magnificent Gothic Library lately built at Stowe, for the reception of the MSS. of that collection.

"You mention, in your History of Leicestershire, (Vol. III. p. 469,) a hill called *Robin-o'-tiptoe*, in the parish of Tilton. Upon the

---

* In the Gentleman's magazine for 1796, vol. LXVI. p. 913, is an engraving of a carving somewhat similar (except that it is in wood) on a chimney-piece in the great parlour of the Tankard alehouse in St. Stephen's parish at Ipswich, formerly the mansion of Sir Anthony Wingfield, K. G. privy counsellor, and one of the executors to King Henry VIII. Part of the building has served as a play-house; and the family chapel opposite thereto is succeeded by Dr. Gwynne's house.

Uninterrupted tradition has referred the Ipswich carving to the Battle of Bosworth. But Mr. Gough, in a letter to Mr. Urban on the subject, says, "Shall I venture to break the thread of that tradition, and say, that it is nothing more nor less than the Judgement of Paris, and its consequence? Paris is seated, habited in his Phrygian robe and bonnet, amusing himself with his lute, when the three goddesses present themselves to him. The next scene is his adjudgment of the prize; when Juno, as Queen of Heaven, leads the way, followed by Venus, disclosing all her charms; and she by Pallas, with the Gorgon's head and ægis. Paris, won over by the attractions of Venus and her assistant son, who is hovering in the air above, adjudges to her the apple, which he holds in his left hand. We next view him, armed cap-à-pie, reclining, perhaps at the foot of the statue of his Patroness, meditating his conquest, his lance lying by him, and his horse saddled and bridled. The reclining warrior and the horse are the only figures in the piece that could possibly suggest the idea of the Battle of Bosworth; but the latter might with equal propriety have been taken for the Trojan horse as for that of Richard III. or Paris for that King. Below, in the left corner, we see Paris and one of his friends prepare with horses to carry off Helen; and in the distance they are seen offering up their vows in the Temple of Venus, or, perhaps, solemnizing their nuptials, the horse or horses waiting without.

"I should be sorry to deprive Lady Lucan or Mr. Hardinge of such a subject for their illuminated Shakspear; but I cannot help thinking the present the more probable illustration.   R.G."

summit is a Fortification, of an oblong square, which I take to be Danish, containing about one acre. There is one Tree within the Camp, in a state of great decay; probably not less than a thousand years old; from this, I apprehend, the Hill took its name of *Robin o' tiptoe*. I have lately purchased the Hill.   W. HUTTON."

Thus far the original Historian of *Bosworth Field*; whose apprehensions, however, that the famous Well where Richard quenched his thirst will sink into oblivion, I am happy to observe,

HENRY VII.

From an Original Painting in the Possession of Lady Bedingfield.

Publish'd by Nichols & Son, Oct 1.1813.

H. Crowe sc

Inscription on

KING RICHARD'S WELL,

IN

Bosworth Field, near Hinckley.—1822.

AQVA. EX. HOC. PVTEO. HAVSTA
SITIM. SEDAVIT
RICHARDVS. TERTIVS. REX. ANGLIAE
CVM. HENRICO. COMITE. DE RICHMONDIA
ACERRIME. ATQVE. INFENSISSIME. PRAELIANS
ET. VITA. PARITER. AC. SCEPTRO
ANTE. NOCTEM. CARITVRVS
XI. KAL. SEPT. A. D. MCCCCLXXXV.

ENGLISHED :

WITH WATER DRAWN FROM THIS WELL,
RICHARD THE THIRD KING OF ENGLAND,
ALLAYED HIS THIRST,
WHILE FIERCELY & WITH DEADLY HATRED,
HE WAS WAGING BATTLE WITH
HENRY EARL OF RICHMOND,
AND WHEN HE WAS DOOMED BEFORE NIGHT
TO LOSE HIS SCEPTRE AND HIS LIFE.
AUGUST 22, 1485.

WARD, PRINTER, HINCKLEY.

are totally done away, by the recent exertions of my profoundly-learned Friend, the Rev. Dr. PARR; by whose indefatigability, intelligence, and erudition, the site of this memorable spot will be handed down to the latest posterity.

In a Letter dated "Hatton, Sept. 13, 1813," which I here use by his express permission, Dr PARR says, "As to Bosworth Field, six or seven years ago I explored it, and I found Dick's Well, out of which the tradition is that Richard drank during the Battle. It was in dirty, mossy ground, and seemed to me in danger of being destroyed by the cattle. I therefore bestirred myself to have it preserved, and to ascertain the owner. The Bishop of Down spoke to the Archbishop of Armagh, who said that the ground was not his. I then found it not to be Mrs. Pochin's. Last year I traced it to a person to whom it had been bequeathed by Dr. Taylor, formerly Rector of Bosworth. I went to the spot, accompanied by the Rev. Mr. Lynes, of Kirkby-Malory. The grounds had been drained. We dug in two or three places without effect. I then applied to a neighbouring Farmer, a good intelligent fellow. He told me his family had drawn water from it for six or seven years, and that he would conduct me to the very place. I desired him to describe the signs. He said, there were some large stones, and some square wood, which went round the Well at the top. We dug, and found things as he had described them; and, having ascertained the very spot, we rolled in the stones, and covered them with earth. Now Lord Wentworth, and some other Gentlemen, mean to fence the place with some strong stones, and to put a large stone over it with the following inscription; and you may tell the story if you please.   Yours, &c.   S PARR."

AQVA. EX. HOC. PVTEO. HAVSTA

SITIM. SEDAVIT

RICARDVS. TERTIVS. REX. ANGLIÆ

CUM. HENRICO. COMITE. DE. RICHMONDIA

ACERRIME. ATQVE. INFESISSIME. PRÆLIANS

ET. VITA. PARITER. AC. SCEPTRO

ANTE. NOCTEM. CARITVRVS

II. KAL. SEPT. A. D. MCCCCLXXXV.

The original Publication of Mr. HUTTON is preserved, in the present Edition, without the slightest alteration; but I have added to it such elucidations as occurred during a long research into the general History of the County of Leicester; and have availed myself, particularly, of the opportunity of annexing some Observations on the important Field of Bosworth, the result of an excursion on the 17th of June 1789, as communicated at the time to one of my Companions in that exploration.

Of the Portraits of the three Monarchs, – that of Edward the Fourth is from an original Painting at Southwick House, Northamptonshire (see Gent. Mag. 1804, vol. LXXIV. p. 997); Richard the Third's is copied from Walpole's "Historic Doubts;" and that of Henry the Seventh is communicated to this Work by my friend the Rev. John Homfray, F.S.A. from a Painting, in distemper, on pannel, formerly belonging to his Mother's Family (that is, to the Parrs,) and now in the possession of Lady Bedingfield. It was etched by Mr. Crowe; and represents the Monarch as young, and a white rose in his hand, with a red one in the centre; and was allowed to be an undoubted original by the late viscount Townshend and Horace Earl of Orford.

November 1, 1813.   J.N.

TESTIMONIES

"No part of the English History, since the Conquest, is so obscure and uncertain, as that of the long-subsisting Quarrel between the Houses of Lancaster and York – 'And it is the more remarkable,' says Mr. Hume, 'that this profound darkness falls upon us just on the eve of the restoration of letters, and when the art of printing was already known in Europe.' But this later circumstance, this recent and great acquirement, and which, in the opinion of that writer, might be expected to have diffused a knowledge of the several occurrences at the period in question, had a totally contrary effect; which effect is thus judiciously accounted for by Sir John Fenn, who observes, 'that, the art of printing being newly discovered, people neglected to multiply their manuscripts, and, being anxious to preserve the history of past times, forgot the present.'

"Mr. Hutton, equally sensible of the defectiveness of our Chronicles, in recording a particular incident of the times, has zealously undertaken to give it the clearness it manifestly wants.

"That part of our Author's performance which comprises the life of Richard, 'till he assumed the regal power,' is intended to set his character in a somewhat amiable point of view. It is chiefly extracted from Buck, Rapin, Carte, Walpole, and Fenn; and is preparatory to his general vindication, or, at least, to an extenuation of the guilty proceedings of which he has been accused by Lancastrian Historians, and also by some others of a later date. The truly ingenious Mr. Walpole was the first who attempted, in a particular manner, to rescue the memory of Richard from the obloquy which had been generally thrown on it. He knew, that to palliate the crimes imputed to the King were to lose the point for which he was contending, and he therefore laboured to prove his innocence – and this in every accusation exhibited against him. Hence, in our opinion, his principal error; for, though he has certainly cleared Richard from several of the murders he has been charged with, there are, notwithstanding, others of which it is highly probable that he was the author, as Mr. Hume has very fully evinced, in a note to the last edition of his History of England, and which is given by way of answer to the 'Historic Doubts.'

"Mr. Hutton does not follow the steps of Mr. Walpole; he attempts not entirely to *exculpate* his 'hero' – for so he styles him – but rather to apologize for his conduct on the plea of necessity*, from the force of his ambition, and from the boldness of his character.

"This endeavour to vindicate the character of Richard, by comparing him with others who have been guilty of equal or perhaps of greater crimes than himself, will not be very satisfactory to the man of reason and virtue. It tends, indeed, to the annihilation of every moral and religious duty. The Tyrant who, after committing three or four murders, shall stop his hand, because his end is fully answered by them, is scarcely less an object of detestation than he who adds to their number in the prosecution of his ambitious schemes."
MONTHLY REVIEW, vol. LXXX. p. 124.

"The two latest Historians of Richard the Third do not concur in their representations of their hero. Mr. Walpole, in his 'Historic Doubts,' vindicates him from the deformities objected both to his person and mind. Mr. Hutton aggravates those of the latter; but admits doubts of the former. This eccentric Writer, whom we have already met with at Birmingham and London, finding nobody, in any age, had described Bosworth Field from ocular examination, because its geography was omitted†, and that Mr. Burton, the Leicestershire Antiquary, who owned and resided on the next lordship to it, and must have conversed§ with many who actually saw the Battle, left no anedoctes of it, made several visits to it in the space of eighteen years." – "Mr. Hutton has traced the march of Richard from Nottingham, August 16, to his camp at the Bradshaws on the 18th, and the sites of the camps of the two competitors, and the two brothers Stanley; and, from their contents, calculated the number of the respective troops, amounting in the whole to not quite 30,000 men. He is as particular in detailing the Battle as if he

---

* "So spoke the Fiend, and with necessity,
The Tyrant's plea, excus'd his dev'lish deeds." MILTON.

† See Mr. Robinson's Map, in p. 116.

§ "Mr. Burton was born in 1575, and the battle was fought in 1485; so that a man must have been 90 to have been born the year of Bosworth fight, and 100 to have been ten years old at the time."

had been in it: but, for want of authorities, we must take his word for it, for it is impossible to follow him with other Authors. Mr. Robinson has described the events astronomically, Mr. Hutton, topographically, by leading us to every scene of action."
GENTLEMAN'S MAGAZINE, vol. LVIII. p. 726.

"The Battle of Bosworth Field, as being decisive of a contest which, during a period of 30 years, had deluged England with the blood of its subjects, is doubtless one of the most memorable events of the kind in this Country. This action has accordingly been described by several Writers, but by none so minutely as the present Author, who is more than an Antiquarian – he is an enthusiast on the subject. Bosworth Field appears to be classic ground with Mr. Hutton; and we speak not without sufficient authority when we affirm, that he has surveyed the favoured object of his researches with an attention, an ardour, and a perseverance, never before displayed by any English Historian or Antiquary. He informs us that he was interested, even from his childhood, in this important event; that he has made several visits, in the space of 18 years, to the Field itself, merely for information and inspection; and that he has likewise made many enquiries into the traditions in the vicinity of Bosworth Field, and found it the most copious source of intelligence."
CRITICAL REVIEW, LXVI. p. 217.

"Mr. Hutton's Battle of Bosworth Field contains a variety of circumstances relating to that important and decisive event, which have been unknown to our other Historians and Antiquaries. His information he has drawn, not only from the best remaining Chronicles of the times, but from repeated visits to the scenes of action, which he has examined with uncommon ardour and attention, and minute enquiries into the traditions of its vicinity. This work is interesting and amusing; and may contribute to the illustration of this dark period of English History."
NEW ANNUAL REGISTER.

PREFACE

Dreadful is the situation of a people, when that martial spirit, which should only be exerted to repel an invader, is divided against itself; when instead of shedding the blood of an enemy, they shed their own.

The House of Anjou furnished to this country, a numerous race of Kings, of heroes, and of savages. The princes of this house, being possessed of abilities, but having no ideas of right, had the address to divide the kingdom, and direct one part to butcher the other. But happy had it been for the nation, could they have united, and expelled that nest of vipers, who diffused their poison, to the destruction of thousands. Something like this really happened at the extinction of the Stuart race. A lesson to future ages.

The quarrel between the roses, is one of the most interesting stories in History, but perhaps none is so defectively related; and the reason is, as Sir John Fenn justly observes, that the art of printing being newly discovered, people neglected to multiply their manuscripts, and being anxious to preserve the history of past times, forgot the present.

Persuaded that the latter part of this important quarrel, the battle of Bosworth, is superficially represented, I have taken some pains in a minute research. This little work will nearly comprehend the history of Richard's short reign.

Whatever omissions I may be charged with, want of assiduity, and enquiry are not of the number. My pursuits, as might be expected, were attended with difficulties. I could not even examine the wood in Bosworth Field, without being repeatedly set fast in the mire; though possessed of two feet, I could sometime use neither. If in searching the rubbish of antiquity, I found an imaginary prize, it appeared so cankered with the rust of time, as to baffle the judgment. I have more than once put a whole family into silent amazement, by the singularity of my errand; by opening a subject, which though constantly under the eye, they had never noticed. I frequently perceived embarrassment, at being unable to give me that information of their own premises, which a stranger might reasonably expect; and have myself stood in an awkward light, while I solicited a gentleman to teach me what he had never learnt. But if I could not always find an answer to my enquiries, I always found civility. Authentic information, of so remote a period, is procured with as much difficulty, by the antiquary, as water in Arabian deserts by the traveller. I have treated my friend with a letter, and myself with a journey, yet all the intelligence derived from both, has been comprized in six words; this evinces, that a work, though small, may be expensive, and that literary emoluments are no part of my pursuit.

As the life of Richard, prior to his sovereignty, is but little known, and that little to his disadvantage, I have given a sketch, in an introduction, chiefly extracted from our best authors, as Hollingshead, Grafton, Buck, Dugdale, Rapin, Carte, Walpole, Fenn, &c. Actions best explain motives.

The Introduction

If we survey the house of Anjou, it will be found, one of the most extraordinary in history. The females possessed the spirit of men, the males, that of heroes: as ripe at fifteen, as the generality of youth at twenty. Active, revengeful, prolific, and daring; they seldom arrived at old age, but seemed willing to destroy each other, when fortune neglected to destroy them.

All agree that the name of Plantagenet signifies a broom-plant; and Buck tells us that *Folk*, head of the family, about a century before the conquest, was enjoined by the priest, as a punishment for his sins, to lash himself with that weapon, from which he acquired its name.

This self-afflicter furnished England with seventy-four male descendants of his own name; fourteen of whom were sovereign princes, who filled the throne three hundred and thirty years. Among whom, only three lived to old age, Henry the Third, Edward the First, and Edward the Third; Five fell by the hand of violence, Richard the First, Edward the Second, Richard the Second, Edward the Fifth, and Richard the Third.

Though a crown is coveted beyond every earthly thing, nay, perhaps every heavenly, and is supposed a remedy for every human woe, yet grief shortened the days of three of the Anjovin Kings, Henry the Second, John, and Henry the Sixth; – The other three, Henry the Fourth, The Fifth, and Edward the Fourth, were cut short in early life.

If we cast a melancholy eye, for we can cast no other, upon the end of this numerous race, till the extinction of the name in 1499, we shall find, that out of seventy-four males, Twenty-one died young, Twenty-four in middle age, Twenty-one by violence, and Only eight saw old age.

If a Plantagenet was destroyed, it was generally by the hand of a Plantagenet; a name always honourable, but frequently dangerous. No family was better acquainted with the axe; and if they shewed no mercy to each other, the stranger could not expect it. They dealt out destruction with a savage hand; hence the nobility and gentry fell by multitudes in the tempests of their wrath.

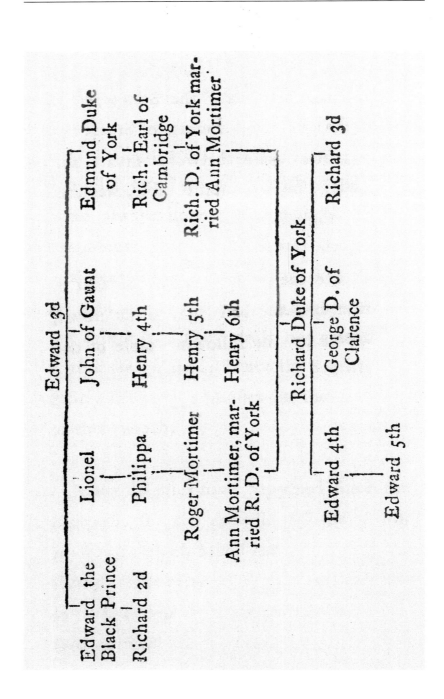

Many disputes have happened since the conquest, for the possession of the crown, in which, much blood has been spilt, and thought right often pleaded, victory carried it. The first dispute arose between the sons of William the Conqueror; the next, between Stephen and Henry the Second; then between Richard the Second, and Henry the Fourth; the houses of Stuart and Orange; and again between Stuart and Brunswick; but the most terrible, was that between the roses.

Whether the house of York, or that of Lancaster had the best right to the crown, will appear by the following table of descent [*opposite*].

It appears from this pedigree, that the house of York could derive no title from Edmund, its founder, because he was the fourth son of Edward the Third. That of Lancaster was equally excluded, because John of Gaunt, the head, was but the third son, therefore the right was vested in Lionel the second, after the heirs of the Black Prince failed; and as the Duke of York married Ann, the heiress of Lionel, the sole right of descent must have been vested in her issue, which was Richard Duke of York. A powerful argument in favour of the Lancastrian family was, their long possession of the crown, which, it was pleaded gave a prescriptive right. But this is a dangerous doctrine; power may preserve that possession which justice cannot ratify. I have observed, upon another occasion, that "whatever is wrong in the beginning, is difficult for time to set right. If a man steals a guinea, it is no more his own, after keeping it twenty years, than it was the first day."

The higher a man is elevated, the more difficult to keep his station. Richard the Second was too giddy to keep his; which, Henry the Fourth, a person of superior talents observing, dragged him from his throne, which he mounted himself. Possession was kept in his family during three generations, when his grandson, Henry the Sixth, a prince much weaker than Richard, was expelled by the powerful Duke of York, the legal heir, a man well able to conduct a kingdom.

Richard Plantagenet, afterwards Richard the Third, was the youngest of eight sons of the last mentioned Duke of York, by Cicely, sister to Richard Neville, Earl of Salisbury, and aunt to the great Earl of Warwick. He was born on Monday, October 2, 1452, at Fotheringay, in Northamptonshire. But little is recorded of his childhood, neither can childhood produce much to record. I shall omit as idle tales, the difficulty of his birth, his being amputated from his mother, his deformity, his savage teeth, and his withered arm, as beneath the notice of history. His infancy was spent in his father's house, where he cuckt his ball, and shoot his taw, with the same delight as other lads.

His father was killed at Wakefield in 1460, Richard being seven years old. His mother sent him, and his brother George, to Utrecht for security and improvement, under the care of Phillip Duke of Burgundy, while their brother Edward, cleared his way to the throne by the sword.

Edward, having subdued his enemies, and ascended the regal seat, sent for his brothers, after an absence of six months, and initiated them into the use of arms, as an additional strength to his house. He created George Duke of Clarence, and Earl of Richmond, to eclipse the title of Henry Tudor, and Richard Duke of Gloucester, and Earl of Carlisle.

There are three incidents in the English annals, which furnished the sovereign with immense property. The seizure of most of the lands in the kingdom, by William the Conqueror, after the battle of Hastings; the assumption of religious donations, by Henry the Eighth, and the prodigious number of estates, alternately seized by the victor, in the contest between the roses. Property was continually changing its owner, according to the victorious sword. This filled the hands of the sovereign with riches, and enabled him to gratify his adherents. To support Richard's ducal character, Edward gave him the fee farm of Gloucester, with the manors of Kingstone Lacy, in Dorsetshire; Richmond in Yorkshire; Chipping Norton in Oxfordshire; Sarton, Great Camps, Abiton Magna and Swaffham, in Kent; Polenthorn, Penhall, Tremarket, Trevalin, Argelles, Trewinion, and Droungolan, in Cornwall; Overhall, Netherhall, Aldham, Preston Pendham, and, Cokefield, in Suffolk; The Castle, and manors of Henham, Elham Parva, Vaur, Bumsted, Helion, Canfield Magna, Stansted Monfitchet, Bumsted upon Terrens, Earl's Calne, Crepping, Bentleigh Magna, Crustwich, Fingrithe, Doddinghurst, Preyeres, Bower Hall, Creyes, Eston Hall, Cileby, Beamond, Downham, – with Kensington, and Walehurst, in Middlesex; Calverton, in Bedfordshire; Milton, and Paston, in Northamptonshire; Market Overton, in Rutlandshire; Fleete, and Battlesmere, in Kent. All which were part of the estate of John de Vere Earl of Oxford, attainted. He also constituted Richard Lord High Admiral of England, Constable of Corf castle, and keeper of the forests in Essex.

The sagacious Edward proposed three advantages to himself by so liberal a bequest. Though this vast property was nominally Richard's, yet Edward would reap the profits during his minority. By parting with it, he would prevent the solicitation of others. He well knew, while a king had anything to give, he would never want beggars, and it would be difficult to deny, even a beggar who had served him. He early saw in Richard a leading capacity, and a rising spirit; he wished to promote his own interest by encouraging both; but alas, he cherished a viper in his bosom; they proved in the end, the destruction of his family.

Three years after, in 1464, Richard being twelve years of age, received a grant of all the castles, lordships, and lands, in England and Wales, late the property of Henry de Beaufort Duke of Somerset, paternal ancester to the present Duke of Beaufort, who having fled at the Battle of Towton, and, being tired with the life of an exile, threw himself at Edward's feet, and obtained a pardon. He afterwards commanded the Lancastrian army at Hexham, where he was taken by the Marquis of Montague, instantly beheaded, attainted, and his estate confiscated.

The interest of the house of Lancaster was, by that victory, for the present annihilated, and the court of Edward enjoyed peace about five years. In 1468, Richard drawing towards sixteen, received a grant of the manor of Fareley in Somersetshire; Haighetsbury, and Cofent in Wilts, with many other lordships, late part of the estate of Robert Lord Hungerford, attainted, likewise, the town of Bodminster, in Gloucestershire, with its dependencies, and all other lands in England, belonging to Alianore Duchess of Somerset, widow of the late Duke, held in dower, which escheated to the crown at her death.

The next year 1469, Richard was made Constable of England, Justice of North and South Wales, and, in 1470, warden of the west marshes of Scotland. Thus he was early taught to rise, who in a few years after was able to teach himself. Had Edward kept him in a dependent state, his wishes would not have soared so high as his present attainments; but being brought *near a king*, he found means to be altogether one. The mind cannot be satisfied; he who has nothing, longs for a little, and, to possess much, only opens a wish for more.

We are now to display another scene, wherein the Lancastrian interest, aided by the powerful Earl of Warwick, grew terrible to the house of York, shook Edward's throne, and occasioned his fall. A proud nobleman, armed with power, has often humbled the crown, but in no instance equal to this. Warwick had placed Edward upon the throne, was his principal support, but taking umbrage at his conduct, forsook him, became his inveterate enemy, and undertook the cause of Henry the Sixth, which he ably conducted. He not only drew his friends after him, but had the address even to draw the king's brother, Clarence; by a bold stroke he drove Edward from the helm, and, by a bolder, took him prisoner. Edward in prosperity lost his prudence, but never in adversity. By a well laid plan he gained one of the greatest blessings upon earth, his liberty; and with a very few friends retreated to the Continent, under the wing of the duke of Burgundy, taking with him Richard Duke of Gloucester, then seventeen. And now, the Lancastrian party, with Margaret at the head, triumphed in a flood of success and of blood.

Edward became an humble solicitor to Burgundy, for aid, to prosecute his fortune, and after an absence of seven months, returned with the assistance of the Duke, marched to London, augmented his forces, and went in quest of the enemy.

Warwick, ready to meet him, marched from St. Alban's and pitched his camp, on Gladmore Heath, a mile north of Barnet. Edward, marched from London, entered the town in the evening, where his people were much inclined to stay and refresh, which he would not suffer, but ordered every man away to the heath. Both armies approached the field the night preceding the action. Edward's came last. Through the darkness of the night, he could not discover the enemy, but by mistake, pitched his camp rather aslant, than opposite Warwick's. He enjoined silence; and fortified his camp as well as time would allow, to prevent a surprize. Both armies had artillery, but Warwick's exceeded Edward's; Warwick played upon the royal army during the whole night, but did little or no execution, for Edward lying nearer than was supposed, the shot flew over him. Each army consisted of about 10,000.

At break of day, Easter Sunday, April 14, 1471, Edward sounded his trumpets to arms, and Warwick drew up in order of battle; but a fog was so thick, that neither party discovered the other. Warwick gave the command of the right wing to his brother, John Neville, Marquis of Montague, who had won the battle of Hexham, but since, changed sides. John de Vere Earl of Oxford, assisted by John Holland, Duke of Exeter, who had married Edward's sister, commanded the left. The centre were archers, under Edmund Beaufort Duke of Somerset, brother to the late Duke. Warwick himself conducted the rear.

The whole van of Edward's army was commanded by Richard Duke of Gloucester, a lad of eighteen; which proves Edward's high opinion of his talents, and confidence in his fidelity. Probably Richard's courage and inclination for the service, induced him to solicit for this dangerous post. Edward, assisted by the Duke of Clarence, whom he had recovered back from Warwick, commanded the second line, in which he placed King Henry, having brought him out of the tower to be shot at. Lord Hastings led the rear. Exclusive of these three lines, Edward had a corps of reserve, for occasional use, which proved of great service.

Edward and Warwick encouraged their men with all the eloquence they were masters of, and each, as usual, pleaded the justice of his cause, the protection of the Almighty, and dealt out abuse against his antagonist.

The thickness of the mist caused another mistake, in preventing the armies from being drawn up face to face. Warwick's left extended towards the east, and far outflanked Edward's right, while *his* left as far overshot Warwick's right.

Soon after the battle began, a small part of Edward's right, being overpowered by Oxford, fled to London, and declared, victory was decided for Warwick. The same fog which had deceived the two armies continued to deceive; Edward's badge being a sun, and Oxford's a star, both with rays, Oxford's mistook their own people for Edward's, and fell upon them, when Oxford cried out "Treason" and fled with 800 men. This disaster did not encourage one party, nor dishearten the other, because neither were able to see it for the mist. The King's people on the west out flanking Warwick, became in turn successful, and routed the enemies right.

The contest had continued till near noon; rather in favour of Edward, which the Earl of Warwick observing, and remembering his character in the world as a hero, and being unwilling to lose his power of making kings, bravely exerted himself, and encouraged others, till the battle became more fierce, and the victory doubtful. Edward, as the last bold effort, brought up his reserve. This no way dismayed the Earl, who still encouraged his people by telling them "it was the last resort of an usurper". But Richard Duke of Gloucester who commanded Edward's van, bore down all before him. It is difficult to withstand a man who is determined nothing shall withstand him. Warwick, inflamed, attempted to do *himself*, what his men were unable. He fought on foot, contrary to his usual practice, and in his ardour for conquest, cut his way into the midst of his enemies, forgetting that he was venturing into the jaws of a boar; surrounded by Richard's people, and his own being too much disheartened to effect his relief, he fell a victim to their fury. The Marquis of Montague, though supposed a friend to Edward, could not bear to see a brother in distress, and in attempting to support him, fell himself. Here opposition ceased.

Thus it appears, when Edward committed so important a trust to his brother Richard, it was not an error of judgment; nor does Clarence seem to have taken umbrage, at being ordered to the centre, while his younger brother commanded the van. The infant sword of Richard had now established that character for bravery, which time cannot efface. John Milwater, and Thomas a Par, two of this squires, were slain at his feet.

There fell on the King's side, the Lords Cromwell, Say, and Pentoise, with many Knights, 'Squires, and Gentlemen. None of the nobility were slain in the Lancastrian interest except the two brothers. The Duke of Exeter was desperately wounded. Somerset and Oxford, attempted to retreat into Scotland, but altering their design, turned towards the left, and marched into Wales, to join Jasper Earl of Pembroke, and the King marched in triumph to London.

An Obelisk was erected by Sir Jeromy Sambroke, upon Gladmore Heath, in 1740 to commemorate the battle, with this inscription:

Here was
Fought the
Famous BATTLE
Between EDWARD
the IVth and the
Earl of WARWICK,
Anno 1471,
In which the Earl
was defeated
and slain.

The keeper at the Red Cow, near the Obelisk, has preserved a ball, a pound and a half weight, which he dug out of the ground.

Though Richard, for the first time, had drawn a victorious sword, he was not yet to sheath it. News was brought to Edward on Easter-Tuesday, that Margaret, with her son, had landed the day of the battle, at Weymouth. Edward staid but four days in London, before he went again with his army, in quest of an enemy. The two antagonists met at Tewkesbury, May the fourth, only twenty days after the battle of Barnet.

Edward, as before, marshalled his troops in three divisions. Over the first, he appointed his brother, the victorious Duke of Gloucester, took the center himself, and gave Lord Hastings the third. Approaching the enemy, he perceived they were entrenched, and could not be attacked, but at a manifest disadvantage. The Queen's army was drawn up in three lines; the first was commanded by the Duke of Somerset, who fled from Barnet, assisted by his brother, Lord John Beaufort. The second, by the Prince of Wales, assisted by Lord Wenlock; and the third by Courtney, Earl of Devonshire.

Edward was provoked because he could not join battle with the enemy, therefore ordered his artillery to open, which did some execution, while Richard continued a brisk discharge of arrows. Somerset in return, played his artillery and small arms with effect, and now might be seen two armies briskly fighting, with a trench between them, Somerset's artillery was inferior to the King's, for the latter had recruited his at Barnet.

As the Duke of Gloucester was not able to reach them with his sword, he was determined to reach them with his policy. Knowing the impetuous temper of the Duke of Somerset, he feigned himself worsted, and, with his van recoiled, as if retreating through fear. This decoy had the desired effect. Somerset left the intrenchment, expecting the Prince and Wenlock to follow, and support him, but neither moved. Richard having drawn him from his strong hold, faced about, and began the attack with double fury, forced him back up the hill, but he could not easily regain the encampment. As Edward approached the Queen's troops, he observed a park full of timber on their right, and fearing an ambuscade, detached 200 spear-men a quarter of a mile to the left to attack them; but if there were none, to employ themselves as occasion should serve. Finding no enemy in ambush, they returned at the very instant Richard was facing about, and joined him. The violent Somerset seeing all was lost, and being in a rage at not being seconded, rode up to Lord Wenlock, upbraided him for a traitor, and at one stroke with his battle-axe, dashed out his brains. The Duke of Gloucester followed his blow with spirit, entered the trench with Somerset, and his followers, when a dreadful carnage ensued. Little opposition seems to have been made, or intended. The appearance of Richard carried terror. While some were running, others were slaying. Unfortunately they to pass a narrow bridge at a mill, near the town; here many fell by the sword, and others were drowned. Of that part who arrived at Tewkesbury, some sheltered in the church, some in the abbey. The ill-fated Edward, Prince of Wales, was taken in his retreat to the town, by Sir Richard Crofts, and closely detained. The King issued a proclamation that "Whoever should bring in the Prince, alive or dead, should have a hundred a year for life, and the Prince if alive be spared." Upon which Sir Richard delivered him up; a fine figure of eighteen. But of Edward's broken promise, and the Prince's fate, I have given an account, *page* 108. This unhappy bud of royalty, cut off from the ancient stem of the Plantagenets, in the spring of existence, had no greater funeral honours paid him, than being thrown into a large hole, in the monastry of Tewkesbury, to ferment and rot with the bodies of common soldiers.

Here fell Lord John Beaufort, Thomas Courtney Earl of Devonshire, Lord Wenlock, Sir John Delves, Sir Edward Hampden, Sir Robert Willington, Sir John Lucknor, Sir William Vaus, Sir Nicholas Harvey, Sir William Fielding, Sir William Lurmouth, Sir John Urman, Sir Thomas Seymour, Sir William Rouse, and Sir Thomas Harvey.

Among the officers who took shelter in the church, were Edmund Beaufort Duke of Somerset, John Strother, Lord Prior of St. John's, Sir Humphry Audley, Sir Gervis Clifton, Sir William Grimesby, Sir William Carey, Sir Henry Rose, Sir Thomas Tresham, Sir William Newborough, Henry Tresham, Walter Courtney, John Florry, Lewis Miles, Robert Jackson, John Gower, sword bearer to the Prince, and ancestor to the present Marquis of Stafford, and James Delves. All these might have escaped, but Edward promised a pardon, upon which they relied. But the event of this second promise, and their dreadful catastrophy, I have mentioned, *page* 94.

Edward, during the last nine months, had experienced a strange vicissitude of fortune. From a powerful monarch, he had been stript of his regal honours, become a desolate wanderer, a prisoner in one place, and his family in another; his life in constant jeopardy, and himself a beggar. He declared, he had lost every idea of a future crown, and only wished to recover his family inheritance. We behold him again, with the aid of Burgundy, rapidly rising to power, taking King Henry prisoner, and, by the assistance of the Duke of Gloucester, gaining two important battles, entirely subduing the house of Lancaster, so that it made little or no efforts for power, during the remainder of his reign. We further behold him, and that with a sigh, glutting his revenge with blood. Provoked at being disturbed after a peaceable possession of the crown for ten years, he slaughtered his enemies without mercy, mangled their bodies, and hung them up in the highways, to the annoyance of travellers. Gloucester did not soften the barbarous spirit of his brother savage.

After the battle of Tewkesbury, Edward had reason to expect a quiet enjoyment of the throne, but he had scarcely returned from the field, when the bastard of Faulconbridge, allied to the Neville family, raised a commotion in Hampshire. The victorious Richard was sent against him in September, came up with, and defeated him at Southampton, took him prisoner, and sent him to Middleham castle, where he was beheaded.

There are but few instances upon record, of a military character, rising to fame with the rapidity of Richard's. Though in law, an infant, in the field an hero. He had fought two battles in three weeks, commanded the van of both, was greatly instrumental in gaining that of Barnet, and compleatly won that of Tewkesbury. This gave him consequence in Edward's court, and, what was much to his honour, he possessed that consequence without its airs.

Edward had given Richard much, but not more than he deserved. In consideration of his merit, he made him Lord Chamberlain of England, and granted him the manors of Middleham, and Sheriff-Hutton, in Yorkshire, Penrith, in Cumberland, and part of the lordships, manors, and lands, belonging to the Earl of Warwick, slain at Barnet; also the estates of Lewis Fitz-John, Robert Harlston, Sir Thomas Dimock, Sir Thomas de la Lounds, John Truthale, John Darcy, and the large estate of the Marquis of Montague.

Richard now at ease, with his sword laid down, was not insensible of the charms of the fair. Two or three natural children were the consequence of this intercourfe, but we are not told by what ladies.

We shall now, in 1473, behold him in another light, a light in which he is seldom placed by the historian, in love. The softest and the most amiable passion of the human heart, is never ascribed to Richard. It was thought by his enemies, if they thought at all, that the tender feelings of a lover, could never enter the breast of a monster. But Richard's disposition was in every respect, like that of other men, two qualities excepted, *Bravery* and *Ambition*. In these he exceeded the run of mankind. The great Earl of Warwick had two daughters, Isabel, and Ann, which last, Buck calls "the better woman," but does not say why. When the Earl had persuaded the weak Clarence to desert his brother's interest, and fly to the Continent, he united him to his own, by giving him Isabel in marriage, and promising half his fortune. Edward Prince of Wales, soon after, married the other. Ann, becoming a widow, by the murder of the Prince at Tewkesbury, and Richard struck with her beauty, paid his addresses; Clarence, like many of the Plantagenets, having no ideas of justice, had seized the *whole* fortune, which he refused to refund, but exerted every effort in his power to prevent the match. This caused a violent quarrel between the two brothers. Clarence fearing Richard would be too powerful, for he who is right, has many advantages over him who is wrong, conveyed the lady away, and hid her so privately that she could not be found. The gallant Richard, with the eyes of Argus, the diligence of Jason, and the assistance of love, like a faithful knight, and true to his injured mistress, neither gave himself or others rest in the pursuit. After many adventures he discovered her, secreted in an obscure place in London, disguised like a servant girl; nay, in the deranged dress of a cook maid. Like the ancient knights of romance, he delivered the fair lady from captivity, and carried her away in triumph. For security he conveyed her to the sanctuary in St. Martin's-le-grand, and soon after led her to the temple of hymen.

The obstinate Clarence still resolving to hold the fortune, the quarrel became serious; Edward, to prevent the consequences, called a parliament, caused the affair to be discussed by the privy council, and undertook himself to be arbitrator. He awarded a portion of the lands to Gloucester, the residue to Clarence, and procured a ratification from the two houses. The amiable Countess of Warwick, mother to the young ladies, gave up her dowry to establish peace in her family. The slightest knowledge in the laws of equity, will convince us that justice was on the side of Richard. If the ladies were joint heiresses, they were each entitled to a joint share; besides, Warwick's promise of half, might have convinced Clarence, he had no right to more. Whether the two brothers were ever cordial friends is doubtful.

By Richard's marriage with the Lady Ann Neville, he had one son, Edward, born in 1474, who died at the age of ten, one year before his father. She has been vehemently accused for marrying the murderer of her husband, consequently, in all her afflictions, unpitied. But this censure did not arise in her life-time, nor till the Tudors had degraded Richard below every degree of truth.

A quarrel happening between the French King, and the Duke of Burgundy, who had married Edward's sister, and the Duke fearing himself too weak to cope with so able an adversary, solicited Edward's assistance. Though the King, towards the close of a short life, was become corpulent, and courted ease, yet, being under obligations to the Duke, for succouring him in distress, and being willing to reduce the power of France, he readily adopted the measure. It had long been a practice of the English sovereigns, to catch at every pretext to fleece their subjects. Edward seized this. He was fond of luxury; always poor, nor is it a wonder, for the frequently feasted the city of London, an expence sufficient to impoverish a richer monarch; but this fashion, like others, has undergone some alteration; whether our modern sovereigns are more proud, or more frugal, or whether the corporation of London has lost its consequence, I leave to others, but their highest entertainment now, at the King's board, is only to sip a little caudle at a gossoping. Edward found means to draw considerable sums from his people, which he called a benevolence, though some people thought the name misapplied; Hollingshed gives us a specimen of his manner. He sent, among others, for an old rich widow, and asked her, with a smile, what she would give towards the prosecution of the war? the lady, struck with his beauty, "for thy lovely face," says she, "thou shalt have twenty pounds." This being twice as much as the King expected, he gave her thanks and a kiss. Perhaps a kiss of any sort had not come near her lips for many years, but she was so delighted with a royal one, that she doubled her offer, and gave him forty.

Nearly all the nobility attended the King in this expedition, many of them holding estates by military tenure. By an indenture of 1474, which conveyed several lordships to the Duke of Gloucester, he was to serve the King his brother, in the wars of France and Normandy, and find at his own expence, one hundred and twenty men at arms, nineteen of which were to be Knights, and a thousand archers.

Edward raised by his frowns, his smiles, and his kisses, the finest army that had been seen in England for some time; we are not told their number, but I judge near 30,000, and led them in person to France. Their rich dresses and trappings, indicated ostentation more than fighting. Whether Edward meant any thing besides parade, is uncertain, for Burgundy and he quarrelled as soon as they met. The French King, terrified at Edward's gallant army, offered him terms, which promoted an agreement.

Some of the principal officers, with Gloucester at their head, who wished to profit by the war, loudly remonstrated against the peace. "We have gained nothing," says the Duke "for all our labour and expence but shame." He afterwards paid a visit to the King of France, who, knowing his great credit with his brother, treated him with the utmost civility. The unsullied army returned to England, with a loss of reputation, but not of blood.

Richard being governor of the northern marches, his residence was at Sheriff-Hutton, in Yorkshire, and sometimes at Nottingham castle. We have in the former part of his life, beheld a war-like character, but in this we shall contemplate an amiable one. The terror of this name prevented northern inroads. All was quiet during his administration. He distributed justice to those who wanted it, and civility to all. By his moderation and probity, he conciliated the affections of the inhabitants. His credit rose to that elevation, and shone with that splendour, as not to set for many years after his death.

He had now gone through about twenty-five years, without a spot. As a legislator he rivalled the sages of antiquity; as a warrior, even without the assistance of any heavenly goddess, he equalled the Trojan heroes. Had some future crimes been avoided, and, had not his character fallen into the hands of the Tudors, who multiplied those crimes, and blew all up into magnitude, he would have stood one of the first candidates for fame.

Perhaps about this time 1477, we may fairly date the rise of his ambition, the time in which he first raised his ideas to royalty. He had been taught to rule; was well qualified; power was bewitching; the crown had a dazzling lustre; he had issue, and he wished to fix it in his family. The unhappy difference between Edward and his brother Clarence, gave Richard the first opening. There is too much reason to think he artfully fomented the quarrel. But this point, like that of fixing upon the perpetrator of a private murder, maybe *believed* easier than *proved*. Thus much is evident, Clarence's faults were rather foolish than vicious. He had committed no crime worthy of death. Edward was strongly persuaded to cut him off, but did not want much persuasions to have saved him. We are not only to blame if we commit a crime, but even if we do not prevent one, when in our power. Richard stood high with his sovereign. He might have been gratified with any favour for asking. One word would have saved Clarence. He did not utter that word.

Clarence left two innocent orphans. An act of attainder immediately passed, to corrupt their blood, and seize their property. This unjust act could not originate from Edward; he had nothing to fear from younger branches; nay, they might rather be future supports to his family. It could not originate from the two houses; they were no more than spaniels who fetched and carried at the command of the crown. Richard must have been the author, because no man living could derive the least benefit but himself; besides, it was part of a consistent plan. There were two families between him and a sceptre, those of his two brothers: he had now disposed of one.

Clarence, no doubt, had entertained some distant hopes of a crown; this appears from two incidents; his blustering words, tending to bastardize his brother, which could only be meant to make a way for himself; and, his agreement with the Lancastrian party, when he left Edward to join them. Henry the Sixth, and his issue, were to sway the sceptre, and upon failure, Clarence, and his. This proves that Clarence had proceeded beyond his right; and the man who will take *a little* of another's, will take more if not prevented. Thus we find three brothers anxious to fill that throne which would hold but one. There was, however, nothing to fear from Clarence, he was too weak a man to carry any point.

In the wars between England and France, the French generally spurred on the Scots to break through all treaties with the English, and make inroads upon the marches. The French, Scots, and Welch, rarely quarrelled with each other, but if England differed with any one of the three, the others, if able, were ready to assist against her. The Picts wall, stands a lasting monument of those barbarous ages; when even in times of peace, all intercourse was prohibited between the two nations. We cannot view this stupendious work, without drawing a comparison between ancient and modern civilization. It was formerly death for a man of either nation to pass this absurd boundary, but now, that friendly intercourse is open which ought ever to subsist between neighbouring beings of the same species. I have contemplated, while standing upon the verge of Offa's dyke, that the ground on each side was the same; the country and prospects the same, that the act of moving the distance of ten yards, could injure no man, nor make a difference in situation, yet it was once lawful, had I passed this short, and innocent space, to have knocked me on the head. As the ground is common, everyone has a right to use it, why then should it be death to the man who treads it? The gentlest founds that once passed this fatal barrier were *Dim Sasneag*, and *Dim cum reag*, but now, the residents on either bank, live as intimately together, as in any part of the island; and I can travel with as much pleasure and safety through Wales, and meet with as friendly a reception, as at home. I can view the grandeur of her mountains without any fear, except that of falling from them.

Whether a coat, or a peace, be slightly patched up, it will quickly come to pieces. Lewis and Edward soon disagreed, and the French King easily prevailed upon James the Third, King of Scotland, to make a descent upon the borders; which he ravaged without mercy, before Edward could form an army. When a King is not prepared for battle, he attempts to negociate. Arbitrators were chosen, by the French and English for that purpose. The Duke of Gloucester was one, and after the usual time of conferring, produced the peace of a day. Treaties between Princes continue, while it is their interest.

Edward having silenced his French antagonist, turned his eye towards Scotland; but the Scots had made such devastations, that forage was not to be found to subsist an army in its march to the North. Richard therefore procured a commission from the crown to purchase

    2000 quarters of Wheat
    1000 do. of Barley
    1000 do. of Rye
    1000 do. of Oats
    1000 do. of Muncorn
    1000 do. of Beans, and
    1000 do. of Pease

With this supply he replenished the marches for the reception of the military. Nor did Richard make any private emolument by this state purchase; *Royalty* was what he coveted, not money. But his dependants knew how to reap the profits of the contract.

Scotland was in confusion. Her King was weak, and the people dissatisfied. He had two brothers. One he had bled to death, the other imprisoned. The living brother, Alexander, escaped from confinement, and fled to England, under the protection of Edward. These two entered into a treaty for which they both deserved punishment. Edward was to dispossess James of the throne; and place Alexander upon it; who was to do homage for his kingdom, to Edward; to break the truce with Lewis, and enter into one with the King of England against him; to divorce his wife, and marry

Edward's daughter; though already engaged to the Prince of Scotland, his nephew; but if the church would not grant a divorce, his son was to marry her. The King's daughter was a forward girl, was early ripe for a husband, and longed for one, as soon as ripe. Her fortune, which was 20,000 marks, had, in part, been paid by Edward's bungling ministers, and the Scots valued the money more than the lady.

Edward having raised an army consisting of 23,000 men, gave the command to the Duke of Gloucester, who began his march, in May 1482, accompanied by Alexander, who assumed the title of King. In July they reached Alnwick. By slow marches they arrived in Scotland and began to lay waste the country, there being no army to oppose them. Richard took Edinburgh, and sent to inform James, "if he did not fulfil his engagements with England, he would destroy the whole kingdom." The nobility of Scotland assembled, ratified the treaty afresh, and delivered up Berwick, when Gloucester with his army returned to England. Nothing memorable happened to Richard during the residue of his brother's reign, which was only a few months.

The death of Edward the Fourth, opened a new, and extraordinary scene, in which Richard shewed himself a most accomplished and wicked actor. There is not in the whole history of the English Kings, a similar instance of a prince forming a design upon the crown, laying so able, and deep a scheme, in which were so many obstacles; surmounting them all, and gaining the beloved object in eight weeks! These obstacles would have appeared insurmountable to any eye but Richard's. He had to overcome Rivers and Gray, with all their adherents, who were powerful, and in possession of the sovereign; the potent friends of Edward's family, as Derby, Hastings, York, Ely, &c. but what was singular, he had the most powerful of all, *the people*. Neither was he assisted in this amazing undertaking, by any person of power except the Duke of Buckingham, who was won by delusive promises, never to be fulfilled. He was the step by which Richard mounted the throne, and then destroyed. The fate of every branch of opposition was determined; the King was committed to prison; Stanley was to be cut off, as if by an accidental blow; the two Bishops seized and confined; Rivers, with the King's friends were solemnly murdered in the face of the sun; Hastings, in a manner unknown in history; and what was astonishing, the people were most unaccountably duped. One circumstance was much in Richard's favour, not one of the heads with which he contended was equal to his own. A bolder display of masterly talents, is no where met with.

Richard being arrived at the regal seat, the ultimate of his wishes, the pinacle of vanity, I shall close this first part of his life, which has been but little noticed by our historians, with an account of his coronation; from George Buck. This was the first author who ever durst speak in favour of Richard. He seems to have written the King's life, or rather, his vindication, about a century after the battle of Bosworth, and says many weak things, and false, but more true. Provoked at Henry the Seventh, for his treatment of Sir John Buck, a near relation, taken at Bosworth, and beheaded with Catesby, at Leicester, he takes a decided part against him, and endeavours to exculpate Richard from every charge. If we cannot find the angel in his description of the King, we find the perfection of man.

When the Duke of Buckingham addressed Richard in the pretended name of the nobility and Commons of England, to take the crown; he shily accepted *that* which he most ardently wished for, and replied with a serious face, "As they were *determined* to make him a King, he was resolved to make himself a good one, and desired to live no longer then while he endeavoured to promote the prosperity of the kingdom." Upon this Buckingham and his followers cried out *God save King Richard*. A discerning spectator must have smiled at the farce.

Buckingham, to serve his master, or rather himself, procured a few addresses, wherein particular care was taken to hint at the bastardy of Edward's children, and the attainder of Clarence's. These were delivered to the Lords, assembled in Westminster-hall, June 26, 1483. Richard sitting among them in a marble chair, or rather upon the celebrated coronation stone, yet preserved in St. Edward's chapel. He was then declared King, and the next day proclaimed. After which he rode in great pomp from London to Westminster, and placing himself in the royal seat, gave a charge to the judges, in a religious strain, to administer justice. He then approached the abbey, and was met at the door by the monks in procession, when the Abbot delivered into his hand, the sceptre of St. Edward. In this manner, he ascended to St. Edward's chapel, and made an offering at the shrine, while the Monks sung *Te Deum*. He afterwards returned in procession to his palace in London.

The man who is fond of power, is fond of parade; this was Richard's case, or why did he travel from Nottingham to Bosworth Field with his crown upon his head? which, by the way, tends to prove a point long disputed, that he was not that misshapen monster he is represented. He who is ill-made would rather *hide* than publish his deformity, and nothing makes a man more conspicuous than a crown.

July 4, he went with his Queen by water, to the Tower, where they slept that night, and the next day, the fifth, he rode with his son from the Tower, through the city to Westminster, in the highest degree of splendour, attended by three Dukes, all that England could boast, for Dukes were not then plentiful; nine Earls, twenty-two Viscounts and Barons, eighty Knights, with an innumerable company of 'Squires, and all the officers of the crown, who were to serve at the coronation. This ostentatious parade, was designed to gratify Richard, and amuse the people, for nothing was transacted except conferring honours. The Duke of Buckingham was called *the glory of the day*, for he out-shone the whole company in the richness of his attire. His horse, and himself were dressed in a suit of blue velvet, embroidered with gold, in imitation of fire, which seemed even to kindle, and flame in the sun. The rich trappings hung to the ground, and, being furnished with gold tassels, were supported, like a pall, by footmen in the most costly dresses. His horse, in this gaudy procession, was taught to be as proud as his rider.

This grand cavalcade arriving at Westminster-hall, Richard created his son, Prince of Wales; invested John Lord Howard with the Garter, and created him Duke of Norfolk; this honour was said to be conferred because he was descended from Edward the First, but *really* because he was a firm friend to Richard. He also made him Earl Marshal of England and High Admiral.

Thomas Howard, his eldest son, was created Earl of Surry, knight of the Garter, and, what is very remarkable, high constable of England, for the day of the coronation only, and at the same time he created the Duke of Buckingham, high constable for life, which he claimed by inheritance. This trifling defect in etiquette seemingly of no moment, was probably the cause of overturning a kingdom, by giving Buckingham the first umbrage, causing his revolt, and raising that tempest which beat down the white rose. The proud spirit of Buckingham could not forgive being denied figuring away, in that important office, upon the most auspicious day, perhaps in his whole life, and being condemned to bear the train of a man, whom he had really created a King! Though he was made high steward for the coronation, yet, while another was carrying a sceptre, a sword, or a crown, before Majesty, he must be consigned to the humble office of *following* and holding the train. The sudden disgust which seized him, points to this as the first cause.

The King created William Lord Barkley, Earl of Nottingham; Francis Lovell, Viscount Lovell, and Lord Chamberlain. Lord Stanley was restored, and made steward of the houshold, Thomas Rotherham, Cardinal, and Archbishop of York, who had been committed for delivering the Great Seal to King Edward's widow, was enlarged and received into favour by the politic Richard, who was sensible of his power.

The King now received the ancient order of the Bath, that he might multiply favours to gratify his friends, and dubbed Edward de la Pool, son to the Duke of Suffolk, his own nephew; George Gray son to the Earl of Kent; William Zouch, son to the Lord Zouch; Henry Neville, son to Lord Abergavenny; Christopher Willoughby; Henry Bainton; Thomas Bullen; William Say; William Enderby; Thomas de Vernon; Lord William Barkley; Thomas Arundel; Gervis de Clifton; Edmund Beddingfield; Thomas Lucknor; William Barkley of Weley Castle in the vicinity of Birmingham; John Brown; and another Gentleman of the name of Barkley. Several of the above knights fought afterwards for Richard, at Bosworth-field.

And now arrived the most happy day in Richard's life, July 6, 1483, a day far surpassing even those in which he lost his brothers, won a bride, or the battles of Barnet and Tewksbury. The Bishop of Rochester led the van of a grand procession, from the Tower to Westminster, bearing the cross; the Cardinal, and the Earl of Huntington followed with the gilt spurs; then the Earl of Bedford, with St. Edward's staff; after them the Earl of Northumberland, with a naked sword without a point, the emblem of mercy; Lord Stanley, with a mace, signifying government; the Earl of Kent on the right, and Lord Lovell on the left, each bearing a sword with a point, emblems of Justice; next, the Duke of Suffolk, who had married Richard's sister, with the sceptre; the Earl of Lincoln, son to Suffolk, with the ball and cross; the Earl of Surry as high constable of England, with the sword of state, in a rich scabbard; the Duke of Norfolk, his father, on his right, with the imperial crown; then followed *the King* in a fur-coat and robe of purple, under a canopy borne by the barons of the Cinque Ports, the Bishop of Durham on his right, and the Bishop of Bath on his left; his train, as above, supported by Buckingham, holding a white staff as High Steward of England, but no mention is made this day of his dress; which is a further evidence that rancour, from disappointment, entered his heart the preceding day.

Then the Queen and her attendants; first an Earl, with the principal sceptre; Viscount Leslie bearing another, with the dove; the Earl of Wiltshire, with the crown; then the Queen, in robes like those of the King, between two Bishops, under a canopy like his, and borne by the Barons: on her head was a coronet, set with diamonds; her train was supported by the countess of Richmond, mother to Henry the Seventh, followed by the King's sister, the Duchess of Suffolk, attended by the Baronesses, and other ladies.

The whole procession entered the west door of the Abbey. The King and Queen only were seated, and the choir sung: then they ascended to the altar, changed their robes, and put on others that were open or slit in various places, to facilitate the idle practice of anointing, which was performed: after this they retreated, and put on cloth of gold, and returned to their seats. The Cardinal Archbishop, assisted by other Bishops, proceeded to the remainder of the ceremony, by putting the sceptre into the King's left hand, the globe into his right, and the imperial crown upon his head. The Queen's sceptre was put into her right hand, that with the dove, into her left. On each side the King stood a Duke, before him, the Earl of Surry, with his sword of state. On each side the Queen, a Bishop, and in front, a lady kneeling. The Cardinal then said mass, and gave the blessing. The King and Queen jointly received the Sacrament, at the high altar. Approached St. Edward's shrine, the King offered up his crown, originally belonging to the Saint, and putting on another, returned in the same state into Westminster-hall, and afterwards retired for a small space.

In the interim came in the Duke of Norfolk, as Earl Marshall, superbly mounted, and covered with cloth of gold to the ground, to disperse the croud in the hall.

The coronation being ended, the King and Queen, about four, sat down to dinner in the middle of the hall. The Queen on his left, attended by two Countesses. On his right sat the Cardinal Archbishop. The ladies were placed at a long table in the middle of the hall, near the King's. The Lord Chancellor and the nobles at another. The Lord Mayor and Aldermen, with Knights, and gentlemen at others.

When the company were seated, came again the Duke of Norfolk as Earl Marshall, the Earl of Surry High Constable, Stanley Lord Steward, Sir William Hopton Lord Treasurer of the Houshold, and

Sir Thomas Percy, Comptroller, all on foot, and served the King's table with one dish of gold, and another of silver. The Queen was served in gilt vessels, and the Cardinal in silver dishes.

During the second course, Sir Robert Dymock, the King's champion entered, mounted and caparisoned with all the ornaments of his office, and proclaimed, "Whoever shall say King Richard the Third was not lawfully King, he would fight him at all hazards;" and, to ratify the engagement, threw down his gauntlet, then the hall resounded *King Richard, God save King Richard*. He repeated his challenge thrice, when an officer of the cellar brought a gilded cup filled with wine, which he drank and carried away the vessel, as his ancient fee. This custom claims its origin from the conquest. Marmion was a powerful Baron, and came over with William, from whom he received many grants, among others, the manor of Scrivleby, in Lincolnshire, to be held by grand serjeantry; that at every coronation, he or his successors, should, as champions, give a challenge at the King's table, and fight any man who should deny his title. The lordship and the office, continued in the Marmions about 300 years, till the extinction of the male line. Coheirs were left; one of them marrying a Dymock, carried both the manor and the office into his family, where they yet remain. Whatever may be the champion's feelings, in this magnanimous challenge, he is as safe on a coronation day, as on any other day. If he was ever in danger, it must have been in challanging *Richard's* title, for no King produced a worse. But if fear seizes him in this tremendous undertaking, he has this comfort, that he hides it under a cumberous helmet.

The Heralds then approached, and after pronouncing the world *Largesse* three times, departed. When the Lord Mayor of London entered, as Lord chief Butler of England for that day, by ancient prescription, attended by the Sheriffs, and served the royal pair with sweet wines; each receiving a gold cup with a cover as a perquisite. By this time, night being far advanced, the company departed, and Richard bid adieu to the happiest day he must ever behold.

If we examine Richard's character, as it then stood with the world, now in his thirtieth year, we shall find in many instances, it appeared in an amiable light. Wherever he resided, he won the inhabitants. His munificence was great; Lord Bacon says "beyond his power." His matrimonial dispute with Clarence, terminated to his honour. As a subject, and a brother, he behaved to his sovereign without reproach. Viewed in a martial light, he stood one of the first of the age. An heroic character is peculiarly pleasing to the English. A name thus established, is not instantly destroyed.

But as a counter-balance, there were three matters against him. His private machinations, destructive to Clarence; although these were so artfully conducted, as perhaps not then to affect his character. The death of Hastings in London, and the noblemen at Pontefract, was another, this however, was too recent to be decided upon with precision. But the most material was his seizing the crown to the prejudice of the legal heirs; for though this unjust proceeding was buried in silence, by the hand of power, it rankled in the breasts of the thoughtful. Thus, upon balancing his excellencies and defects, he could not stand ill with the people at his sham election.

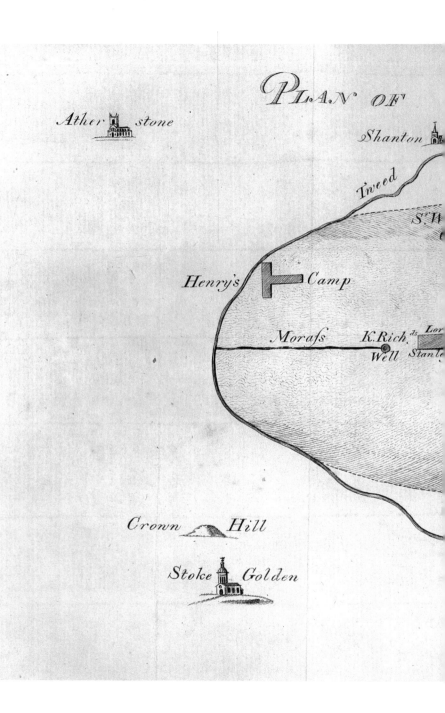

Atherstone

PLAN OF

Shanton

Tweed

S.W

Henry's Camp

Morass   K.Rich   Lor
Well   Stanle

Crown   Hill

Stoke Golden

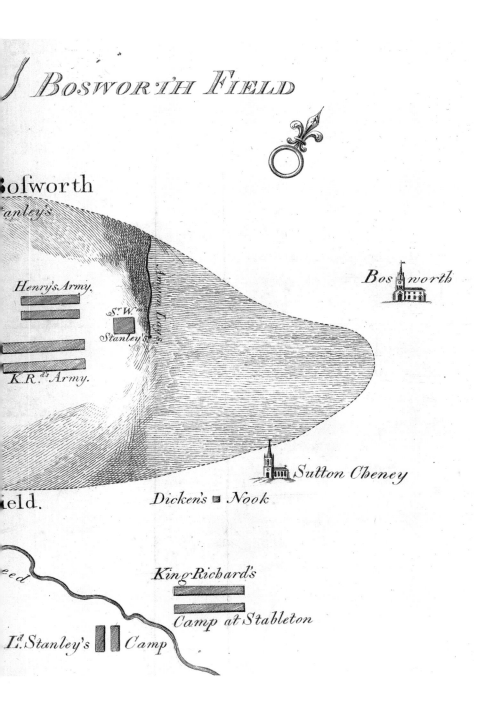

BOSWORTH FIELD

Bosworth

Stanley's

Henry's Army.

Sr. W.
Stanley.

K. R.ds Army.

Bosworth

Sutton Cheney

Dicken's Nook

Field.

King Richard's

Camp at Stableton

Ld. Stanley's Camp

The Battle, &c.

Man, as an intelligent animal, is continually in quest of events, and marks them with value according to their magnitude. Some of the most interesting we know are military contests. Very few pieces of history demand more attention than the description of a battle. When the lives of thousands, the change of property, and the fate of empires are at stake, no wonder our thoughts are captivated. It follows, the more material the action, the more faithful ought to be the description.

Battles are singular periods; productive of strange events. Much may depend upon a trifle, the effects of a trifle may be victory, and the effects of victory, everlasting.

The battle of Bosworth was the last of thirteen between the houses of York and Lancaster; and though it was one of the least, it was of more consequence than the other twelve; nay, the revolutions it caused, were of greater moment than those of any other, since the conquest, for it produced a change in the constitution. Villanage was abolished, the feudal system overturned, commercial treaties were ratified, a spirit of industry encouraged, a flow of wealth was the result, and a kind of equality was established among men.

I must however, intreat the reader's pardon for troubling him with a battle after a lapse of three hundred years, and which has been described by a multitude of historians. He may reasonably suppose, all that can be said upon this subject, has been said ages past. – But if the peruses with attention, the various authors upon this important point of English history, the following observations will naturally occur – That this battle was never described by an eye witness; nor is it at all surprising, for the private men were as illiterate as the Wednesbury colliers, and perhaps but few of the officers were able to write their names, ignorance, and its companion prejudice, were the characteristics of the day – That, as it originally was fabricated upon hearsay, every subsequent writer, without much enquiry, followed his leader – That it never was described in any age, by one who had seen the field, because the geography is omitted. — That every describer appears fond of the wonderful. They tell us among other remarkables, of broken armour being found of an enormous size, as if the strength of that age surpassed that of the former. I have seen some, which differ very little from the present, this inclines me to question, whether the wonder-finders might not mistake the head of a spear for that of an arrow – The historians, agreeable to the fashion of the first age, were all favourers of the house of Lancaster. Rapin seems the first who made the remark; hence the house of Tudor is placed in a more amiable light than it deserves, and black as Richard's character was, he is placed in a more detestable; thus we are deceived with a superficial and random history – They also abound with doubtful and contradictory assertions, some alleging, that Henry was not secure of the Stanleys; that he was obliged to pass a morass; that both armies entered eagerly upon the action; that Richard personally knew Henry; that Henry bravely attempted to close with Richard and kept him at Sword's point; that Sir William Stanley brought into the field 5000 men; that Lord Oxford, who commanded Richmond's main body, confined the whole front line within the compass of twenty feet; that 4000 men fell in the action, but only ten of these were Richmond's; that Richard was a little, ugly, feeble, crooked fellow; and that finding all was lost, he rushed into the heat of the battle, that he might not survive the defeat; that his wretched body contained the soul of a devil, and his followers were scoundrels; all which are mistakes.

Nor have I ever met with a writer who entered into the subject, or had ever given it his thoughts. The least part of my information was derived from those, who, having professedly treated of the battle, ought to have furnished the most. Our expectations are heightened when we peruse Burton's history of Leicestershire, and find he had every advantage for information; nay, perhaps was the only author that had. He owned, and resided upon the very lordship adjoining the famous field; might have leisurely surveyed the scene, and contemplated the actions performed upon it; had beheld many of the curiosities found on the spot; lived near that period, and personally knew many who actually saw the battle. He might have been master of all the traditions of the country; and able to form a complete system of that singular event, and convey it to posterity. But how is the expectation disappointed, when his description of that memorable contest which changed the face of things, amounts to nothing! It is owing to this I write. If he ever surveyed the field it was with inattention. If he acquired historical anecdotes, he lost them as he found them; that which is ever in view, is seen without regard – This laborious, and intelligent author, who was able to give us the best relation, has given us one of the most defective.

Interested, even from childhood, in this important event, I enjoyed a pleasure in enquiry. By carefully examining every author I could meet with, I learnt all they knew. – I have made several visits, in the space of eighteen years, to the field itself, merely for information, and inspection; I have also made many enquiries into the traditions in the vicinity of Bosworth Field, and found this the most copious source of intelligence. Though much was lost, much was preserved. If some of the remarks I met with, were crude and contradictory, yet sometimes one little hint ignorantly dropt, set many uncertainties to rights. If new difficulties arose, I read, thought, and travelled for a solution. By carefully comparing the writers, the field, and the traditions, I have attempted to remove some absurdities and place truth on firmer ground. He who has the advantage of three lights ought to see more distinctly than he who has but one.

I do not, however, pretend to enumerate every fact, or warrant the truth of every word; for it must be considered, the period is distant, and many incidents which are material, and would elucidate others, are buried in time. In some parts of the road, I am obliged to follow the footsteps of my predecessors. Where they treat of the interests of Richard or Henry, they must be followed with caution, but where those interests are out of the question, they are much safer guides. When I quit their path, and follow my own, I shall be attentive to punctuality. In history, as in mathematics, from one known position another maybe drawn; and from two that are wrong, may sometimes be drawn a right. Truth is the grand mark of the historian; he who says the best things, says the truest.

The prince who possesses a throne by unfair means, finds it an uneasy seat. This was the case with William the First, with Stephen, John, and Henry the Fourth. That right was wanting which is ever necessary to secure a firm possession. But of all defective titles, that of Richard the Third seems the worst, and his reign the most uneasy. We know of but two lawful roads to a crown, the choice of the people, and an hereditary claim; that of conquest being no other than a robbery; he possessed neither. It is surprizing that Richard, who was a man of sense, and an able reasoner, should so far forget himself, as to cast an eye upon a diadem while there were ten persons before him, exclusive of Edward the Fourth who held it, all in youth and health. But if we examine his unboundless ambition, the surprize ceases. Though his body was small, that ambition grew to a gigantic height, and attempted to overlook ten heads. He shrewdly judged, if he could acquire power, it would be no difficult thing to cut those heads shorter. I doubt not, but his conscience would have suffered him to destroy one half of the kingdom, to have swayed the sceptre over the other. A predominant passion is a bold trait in some characters; favourable incidents occur, which draw this leading power into action. The love of *liberty* was the grand feature in the great *Hampden's*, and this was called forth by his elevated station. Had he been in an humble sphere, he would have been no more than the barber of the village – *Cruelty* shone with dreadful lustre in the famous Kouli-Khan's; which, had he held the plough, instead of the sword, would have displayed itself in hanging dogs, whipping horses, torturing flies, watching for sentence at the Old Bailey, or following the judge on his circuit; the ruling passion of Henry, after he grasped the sceptre was *avarice*. Had he moved in a servile state, he would like other misers, the dregs of existence, have denied himself common support, dined upon offals, and his small savings would at his death, have been found in a rag. And Richard's was *ambition*. This is a laudable passion when guided by reason, but being possessed in the extreme, and under no controul; it proved destructive to many, and in the end to himself.

But ambition would have lain dormant for ever, even in Richard, and his character been saved, but for the assistance of Henry Stafford duke of Buckingham, a man of florid abilities, much power, and more pride; who, like the great Earl of Warwick, expected to make and unmake kings at pleasure, he alone set the crown on Richard's head; not out of love to the king, but himself. Buckingham thought, like other men, his wages could not be too great, and Richard thought the same, before the work was done; but there is nothing more common than to throw by a tool which has performed all we wanted. How far these degraded characters had driven a bargain, never fully appeared to the world; but all agree, and with reason, that Buckingham wished a moiety of the Hereford estate, vested in the crown, and Richard cherished the wish. Perhaps he solicited for the whole, and was disappointed by receiving only a part – Humphry Bohun Earl of Hereford was immensely rich, possessing more than forty lordships, about 2300*l*. per annum. He had two daughters; Ann married to Thomas Duke of Gloucester, son of Edward the Third, and Mary, to Henry the Fourth, grandson to

Edward; the uncle and the nephew married two sisters. Ann was great grandmother to the Duke of Buckingham. As co-heirs, they divided this vast fortune. Richard the Second, after the murder of his uncle Gloucester, took his effects, and the whole became the property of the crown, till the death of Henry the Sixth, when that line expired; all the estate therefore ought to have reverted back to the heirs of Ann, consequently Buckingham had a right to all. For though Richard the Third succeeded to the throne, he could not succeed to the private property of a former king. Buckingham took umbrage. When one man serves another in a base cause, the reward frequently produces disgust, and disgust, by artful management, may be blown into wrath, as a spark into a flame.

During the protectorate of Richard, John Morton, Bishop of Ely, an able chancellor, but an enemy to the protector, had been arrested, and committed prisoner to Brecknock castle, under the care of Buckingham. Perceiving the duke dissatisfied, he by insensible degrees, improved that dislike into revenge. He represented the tyranny of Richard; the dreadful effects of civil wars, with which England had long been afflicted, and pressed the duke in his great wisdom to find out a cure. Moreton himself had found the remedy, and darkly pointed it out to the duke that he might have the credit of the invention, which would the better secure his assistance.

Between the duke and the prelate, one of whom had power, the other a head, it was agreed, that the duke's interest should be thrown into the Lancastrian scale; that the Earl of Richmond, heir of that house, should marry Elizabeth, heiress of that of York, his fourth cousin, which would put a period to blood; and that the friends of both, should unite in deposing Richard. The scheme was relished by all parties, and Moreton was suffered to fly to the continent to promote it.

Richmond had long been an exile at Vannes, in the Duke of Brittany's dominions, to avoid the vengeance of the house of York. Edward the Fourth wished to have him in his power, to prevent any future operations against his family, but alas! how little can we foresee events? He never imagined, the greatest enemy to his family was his own brother at home! – Richard suspected this matrimonial design, and took the measures of an able statesman to prevent it.

The Duke of Brittany furnished Henry with men, money, and ships, to make a descent on the West of England, where he was to be aided by the Courtneys, and their adherents. The Duke of

Buckingham also, was to join them with a body of Welch, but events were unfavourable to their scheme, and seemed to unite in securing Richard on the throne – Richmond's fleet was dispersed in a storm, and himself in the utmost danger of being taken prisoner. Buckingham, who meant to pass the Severn at Gloucester, was prevented by the greatest inundation ever known. It lasted ten days; during which time, the country not being able to furnish his Welch army with provisions, nor he with money, it mouldered away, while the Duke with one servant, was obliged to hide himself from the man he had lately armed with power and then offended. The confederacy in Devonshire and Cornwall, terrified at his disaster, disappeared without a blow; the private men laid down their arms, some of the gentlemen fled, others were taken and executed; among whom, was Sir Thomas St. Leger, who had married Richard's sister, the Duchess of Exeter. All this happened in October 1483, only four months after the Duke had set the crown on Richard's head. Destitute of relief, and of safety, the unfortunate Duke recollected an old servant, who owed him many obligations, named Ralph Bannister, of Lacon-hall, near Wem, in Shropshire, the ancient seat of the Bannisters, to this gentleman he fled in disguise for shelter. Richard offered a thousand pounds for discovering him, and Bannister, either for fear of Richard's resentment, or love of his reward, discovered him to John Mitton sheriff of the county; who, with a posse, surrounded Bannister's premises, and seized the Duke, disguised like a peasant, in a old piled black cloak, and hid in a little orchard, near the house – He was conducted to Shrewsbury, where Richard then kept his court, and suffered to live while he confessed all he knew, but not to use any means to save his life, for he earnestly entreated to see the king, that he might plead his past services, which were unparalleled, or offer his future, which might still be great, and also his alliance of blood, for they were both descended from Edward the Third in the fifth degree; but this was denied. For Richard considered *that* power was too great to be trusted with any man, which was able to make a king! For which reason he could not be forgiven, therefore expressly ordered Mitton to behead him, on Sunday Nov. 2d. in Shrewsbury market-place. This was performed upon the spot, now covered by the butter-cross, at the top of Pride-hill, where, eighty years before, Percy, Earl of Worcester, Trussell, Lord Kinderton, and Sir Richard Vernon, were beheaded by Henry the Fourth when Hotspur fell – thus Richard acquired stability by misfortune, a well laid plan was destroyed by the floods, and Buckingham lost his life by a king of his own creating. But Hollingshead tells us that Bannister, who had betrayed his master, never received a shilling of the thousand pounds; for which, Richard is said to have given this reason, "that he did not deserve it. For the man who had betrayed so good a friend, would betray any one else." But, perhaps, a better reason was, that the king had not a thousand to give. He was constrained through mere poverty, to sell the crown plate, a few months before, consisting of 275 pounds, 4 ounces, for 3s. 4d. an ounce, to pay a body of 4000 sorry troops, hired from the North, to secure his coronation. But the truth is, he gave Bannister the manor of Yalding in Kent, late the Duke's, to hold by knight's service. Bannister possessed this lordship about eighteen months, when Henry the Seventh rescinded the grant, seized the manor, and restored it to Buckingham's son, the legal owner.

Whether the Duke was privy to the murder of Edward the Fifth and his brother, will for ever remain a secret; but I suppose he was not, because Richard durst not venture to disclose an affair of so vile a nature, to the first subject in the kingdom, which must have been opened with caution even to a common rascal; neither was his assistance necessary. Works of darkness are best performed by a few; besides, he had already done more for Richard than the earldom of Hereford was worth, and all that Richard could bestow. Nor was private murder any part of the Duke's character, which was composed of choler, ambition, honour, and revenge.

While Henry remained at Vannes, we behold a curious political picture, of a prince and his minister, or if you please, a master and servant, in the persons of the Duke of Brittany and Peter Landoise, both striving which should make his market of Henry, a young captive; and we behold two able politicians, in the persons of Richard and Henry, circumventing each other for a crown. They both knew as well as Sir Robert Walpole, that every man had his price, and that he who is possessed of the means of temptation, may easily carry his end. Henry having nothing to give the servant but the empty promises of a future king, of no weight with a foreign subject, was not able to establish a contract. But the case was otherwise with the master, he received Henry's promises as currency, and in turn engaged to assist him. On the other hand, Richard not giving the master so much as Henry promised, was not able to succeed; when, like the sons of Jacob, he attempted the servant, and not only carried presents, and money in the sack's mouth, but even filled the sack, which instantly won him. Richard was to give Landoise all the annual profits arising from the earldom of Richmond, and Landoise, on his part was to deliver the Earl a prisoner to Richard – Thus the king of England, and the minister of Brittany, famous for cunning, outwitted Henry, though a match for both, and thus the Duke, like many a sovereign prince, was a cypher in his own dominions, and Landoise, like many a servant, governed his master.

This treaty would have been fatal to Henry had not his faithful friend, the Bishop of Ely, discovered it, and apprised him of his danger. He instantly departed privately, but we are told, he had not quitted the Duke's dominions one hour, before Landoise's people arrived at the spot.

Richard, having penetrated to the bottom of Henry's plan, to marry Elizabeth, and unite the two houses against him, instantly saw his own ruin. He wished to frustrate the scheme, and as he could not break it by getting the Earl into his power, he seemed determined to break it by marrying Elizabeth himself. This would have been too difficult for any man to accomplish, except Richard, for he had already a wife. Henry, chagrined at the loss of a future bride, or rather, a future crown, attempted to marry the sister of Sir Walter Herbert, a powerful Welchman; and as the Earl of Northumberland had married another sister, he expected to unite two potent families with his Lancastrian friends, to assist him in mounting the throne. Henry, to whom the whole sex was indifferent, was so fond of royalty, he would have sacrificed domestic happiness, and married even a mother Shipton, or a witch of Endor, for a crown; and Richard equally fond, would freely have consigned his soul to eternal perdition.

Driven from the court of Brittany, Henry applied to that of France, under Charles the Eighth, was received with kindness, and spent near two years soliciting succours, for another attack upon the crown. A man of less ambition, and less penetration than he, would have given up every thought of a future attempt, and considered, from the ill success of the last, the fates, and the elements were against him. However, in July 1485, he accomplished part of his wish, and obtained a small *crew* of men. Phillip de Commins, who saw this crew, declared them the worst he had ever beheld, and undeserving the name of soldiers. They were the scum of the French nation, the sweepings of gaols, hospitals, and the streets, and sent to England, as we formerly sent people to America, afterwards to the hulks, on the Thames, and now to Botany-bay. They are charged with bringing over that dreadful scourge, called the *sweating sickness*, which sorely afflicted this country like the plague, for half a century.

It is not in the nature of court policy for the French heartily to assist the English. By faint assistance, discord is promoted and a rival kingdom weakened, so that all fear of opposition is dispelled. While we tear each other to pieces, as in the contest between York, and Lancaster, and between Charles the First and his parliament, the French look silently on. If we do the dreadful work ourselves, there is no need of their help. Interference would only promote a union, as in the barons wars, in the beginning of Henry the Third. But if a competitor arises, as in the case of the Chevalier, in 1715, and in that of his son, in 1745, they may amuse with promises, but it is their interest to throw in no more fuel than will keep up the flame. Religion may be the pretended motive, but the French will never quarrel with the English for being protestants, but for being powerful; they have by silent steps, for many years, been turning protestants themselves.

In all disputes determinable by the sword, both parties appeal to the people as the ultimate source of strength. Charles the First on one side, and the House of Commons on the other, attempted this great acquisition, by repeated addresses. Stephen, being able to win the people, won the crown; and James the Second, for want of that ability, lost it. That ingenious antiquary Sir John Fenn, who calls back departed ages, and brings the distance of 300 years as perfectly to view as yesterday, gives us a curious letter from Richard to the people of England, dated at Westminster, June 23, 1485, wherein he artfully persuades them "to resist Henry Tudor, and his attainted traitors; whom he pronounces murderers, adulterers, extortioners, rebels to God, honour, and nature; who obey his ancient enemy the French king; and under Henry their bastard leader, begotten in double adultery, intend to enter his kingdom, and, by conquest, dispoil his subjects of life, liberty, and goods; to destroy all the honourable blood in the realm, and seize their possessions, therefore advises every man to lift up his hand against them. He tells them the French king lends assistance, in consideration of Normandy, Anjou, Mayne, Gascoign, Guysnes, Cassell, Hams, Callis, and the marches being given up, and the arms of France for ever being dissevered from those of England; and that Henry had already bestowed upon the enemies of the kingdom, the bishopricks, and spiritual dignities, with the duchies, earldoms, baronies, and inheritances of knights, esquires, and gentlemen; that the old English laws are to be abolished, and those of a tyrant established among the people. That Henry Tudor and his wicked followers will commit the most horrid murders, slaughters, and robberies, that ever were heard of in a christian country; every true Englishman therefore, is commanded to furnish himself with arms, to oppose the rebels, in defence of his wife, children, and possessions; and the king himself will courageously expose his most royal person, to every labour and hazard, to subdue their enemies, and comfort his faithful subject; and calls forth every man to defend his king in battle."

Two powerful weapons may be employed against an enemy, the pen, and the sword; Richard was master of the two. The sword is supported by courage, and skill; he had both. The pen conquers by truth, and ability, here he had but one, for his whole fabric being founded in falsehood, it could not be aided by truth. – Richard had evidently three points to carry in this circular letter, to depreciate his antagonist, to persuade his subjects that the invaders were more *their* enemies than *his*, and, by terrifying the people, to crowd his standard.

Schemes of human invention acquire credit or discredit, not according as they are well or ill-laid, but according to their good or ill success. No plan could be better formed than that of Henry and the Duke of Buckingham to join in the West. None could succeed worse. Of all the ill-laid schemes we meet with in history, none was more absurd than that of William the Conqueror's making a descent upon this country, and yet he is never censured by our historians because it proved successful. Lord Bacon says "there is nothing easier than to direct, blame, or applaud, when a thing is past, nothing harder before it is begun." Richard was the deepest politician of the age, Henry excepted. His wicked plans were well laid, and cautiously executed. If they ever miscarried, it was not owing to himself, but to those he was obliged to trust. He is accused for want of prudence, in not opposing to the two Stanleys a body of men; as his army was nearly equal to Richmond's, and both theirs; but this is a false accusation as will afterwards appear. The same objection is exhibited against him for laying up his ships after Henry and Buckingham miscarried, and with some reason; for had his fleet continued to traverse the seas, Richmond would have found a second attempt difficult. But even this oversight admits a powerful excuse. Richard knew he already stood ill with his people, that nothing soured them like taxes; and as a fleet could not be supported without, he was unwilling to burden them. Thus necessity made a bad man a good king.

Sunday, July 31, 1485, we behold Henry at the head of his *crew*, consisting of 2000, set sail from Harfleur, and on Saturday the 6th of August, arrive at Milford Haven. He marched through Wales, by Dell, Haverfordwest, Cardigan, New-Town, and Welch Pool, to Shrewsbury.

As he designed for London, we may be surprized at first view, why he took this indirect road? But Henry's sagacious head furnished many weighty reasons. He was of Welch name and extraction, was descended from the ancient British kings, had many relations, and great interest there; and the farther he passed through that country, the more strength he would gain. He was more likely to command a passage over the Severn at Shrewsbury, than either at Bristol, Chepstow, Gloucester, Worcester, Bewdley, or Bridgnorth. He might also, from the fate of the unfortunate Buckingham, wish to avoid the Severn at a broad water; besides, as the Stanleys were northern gentlemen, they could the easier assist him. – The scheme answered, for he was joined by many powerful chiefs; as Richard Griffith, Arnold Butler, John Morgan, Sir Walter Herbert, Rice-ap-Thomas, &c. each with a little army.

He was at first denied access into Shrewsbury, by the bailiff, Thomas Mitton; of the same family as he, who two years before, had faithfully served Richard, as sheriff for the county, in seizing, and executing the Duke of Buckingham. In this gentleman, we behold the true nature, consequence, and bounds of an oath. He had willingly sworn fealty to Richard; but finding it inconvenient to keep his oath, cunningly devised a way to save his credit, and cheat the Almighty. I shall relate the anecdote in the words of an old author, quoted by Phillips. "When the Earle of Rychmoond came to the Towne of Shrosberie the gates were shutt against hym and the pullys let downe; so the Earl's messengers came to the Welch gate commanding them to open the gates to theyre right Kynge. But maister Myttoon made answere, being head Bayley, and a stoute royste gentleman, saying, that he knew no Kynge but only Kynge Richard, whose lyffetenants, he and his fellows were, and before he should enter there, he should goe over hys belly, meaning thereby, that he would be slayne to the grounde, and so to run over him before he entered, and that he protestyd vehemently upon the oathe he had tacken; and so the sayd Earle returnyd with hys companye back againe to a vylledge callyd Forton 3 myles and a halfe from Shrosberie, where he lay that night, and in the mornyng followyng, there came Embassadores to speak wyth the Baylyff, requesting to passe quyetlye, and that the Erle theyre maister dyd not meane to hurte the towne, nor none theroyn, but to go to try hys ryght, and that he promysed further, that he would save hys othe, and hym, and hys fellows harmlys. Upon thys they entered, and the sayd Myttoon lay along the grounde wyth hys belly uppwards, and soe the said Erle stepped over hym and saved hys othe." – The loser is the rebel. Had Buckingham been fortunate, instead of suffering by the axe, *he* also might have stepped over Mitton's belly.

Richard having information that a storm was gathering, but not knowing where it might fall, kept his court at Nottingham castle, the centre of the kingdom, that he might not be far from the scene of action. But his late success, and his having secured the princess Elizabeth, made him despise the Earl, and consider his attempts as madness. And though he suspected many of his nobles; yet, since Buckingham's defeat, he could not find one able to give him disturbance. Though hated, it was by men of little power.

Lord Stanley seemed to stand first in his suspicions, but was much inferior to the Duke. He had been firm to Edward the Fourth, and afterwards to his children; had gone every length with his friend Hastings, in favour of the protector, even to the butchery of the queen's relations, at Pontefract; but he could not consent to Richard's mounting the throne at the expence of the young princes; therefore Richard ordered him to be dispatched by one of the ruffians, with a battle-ax, as if without design, at the council board, when Hastings fell, but he escaped destruction by sinking under the table. – He had also married the Countess of Richmond, mother to the Earl, and when he desired to quit the court upon private affairs, Richard obliged him to leave his eldest son the Lord Strange, as an hostage for his future conduct. This important pledge convinced Richard, that Stanley durst not act against him were he willing. – There is nothing easier than for a man to reason himself into security.

But as a cautious man, among enemies, should be ever on his guard, he sent to Herbert and ap-Thomas, to oppose the Earl, with all their power, if he came that way. He also ordered his distant friends to be in readiness, and stationed post horses at every twenty miles, to facilitate intelligence.

Richard was fond of Nottingham castle, often resided there, had erected a turret on the eminence, where the present castle stands, and called it *the castle of care*. While he kept his court there, he endeavoured to gain the friendship of the neighbouring gentry, and persuaded several to join him; particularly Sir Gervis Clifton, whom, at his coronation, he had created Knight of the Bath.

As the Earl marched with expedition, the first certain news that Richard heard was, that the Welchmen had not only suffered him to pass unmolested, but even favoured his pretensions, and that he was arrived without molestation, at Shrewsbury. Here Richard's affairs took a serious turn, he perceived his friends were forsaking him, that they promised much, and did little; his prognostications were unfavourable, anger and vengeance united in his face, his good humour fled and never returned.

The king sent for the Duke of Norfolk, the earl of Surry, and the Earl of Northumberland, to join him, and ordered Sir Robert Brackenbury, lieutenant of the Tower, "to bring Sir Thomas Boucher, and Sir Walter Hungerford, with all the forces they could instantly muster;" for as he thought Richmond would pursue his road to London, by the Wattling-Street, he resolved to meet him and give him battle.

The uncertainty of the place where Richmond would land, and the rapidity of his progress, rendered it impossible for Richard to complete his forces. His friends were scattered, because he knew not where to assemble them. None of the above commanders were with him at Nottingham. Norfolk, Surry, and Brackenbury, probably joined him at the camp, at Stableton, and Northumberland at the field. *Fenn* gives us a short, but curious letter from the Duke to Sir John Paston, sheriff of Norfolk and Suffolk, which, though without a date, must have been written, only a few days before the battle, wherein he tells the sheriff, "that the enimy was landed, that the king would march on Tuesday August 16th, and that he himself, the same night should rest at Bury (St. Edmunds) in his way to the army, and desires the sheriff to meet him at Bury with the men he had promised the king, and bring besides, as large a company of tall men as he could procure, dressed in jackets of the Duke's livery, and he would reimburse his expence, when they met."

It appears from this letter, which was perhaps the last he wrote, that the uniform of the royal army was the jacket, and the colour of each party, was the livery of their chief.

Whether Paston joined the Duke at Bury is uncertain, but from the shortness of the time, I suppose he did not; and besides, a year after, he was employed by Henry, to seize Lovell as a traitor, which supposes, Henry did not think *him* one.

Henry made no stay at Shrewsbury; he wisely judged that lingering would weaken the spirit of enterprize, and diminish his army. Though possessed of no personal courage, he wished to strike, and not wait to be struck.

Leaving Shrewsbury, he encamped at night on a little hill by Newport, when Sir Gilbert Talbot, sheriff of Shropshire, uncle, and guardian to the Earl of Shrewsbury, a minor, joined him with 2000 men, the power of their house with that of his office.

He arrived at Stafford, where he and Sir William Stanley had a private interview, not so much on his own account, as his brother's, who durst not appear because of his son.

At Lichfield he passed the night in his camp, without the walls; and next morning was joyfully received into the town, which the Lord Stanley, two days before, had evacuated as if flying before him.

The king hearing Henry was encamped at Lichfield, would have marched on Monday August 15, but that day being the assumption of our lady, perhaps through fear of becoming unfortunate, by incurring her displeasure, he deferred it till the 16th, when he marshalled his troops in Nottingham market-place, and marched them in exact order, to Leicester, twenty-five miles distant, where he probably arrived the same day, chusing rather to rest his men after a fatiguing march, than fight them after an easy one; besides, time was necessary to take measures. They chiefly consisted of foot, which he separated into two divisions; the first marched five in a rank, then followed the baggage, then himself, gorgeously dressed, upon a large white courser, richly caparisoned, attended by his body guards; afterwards, the second division, five a breast, as before. The horse also being divided formed the wings, and kept near the centre.

This ostentatious parade was to shew his power to the greatest advantage, to deceive the eye, and intimidate the enemy. Richard's wire-drawn army, would cover the road, at least three miles; they would be more than an hour in marching out of Nottingham, and as long in entering Leicester, so that to a common observer, his numbers would seem prodigious. His countenance all the way indicated a troubled mind, and his words declared vengeance. He entered Leicester in all the pomp he could assume, a little after sun set.

In the north-gate street, yet stands a large handsome half-timber house, with one story projecting over the other, formerly an inn, the *Blue Boar*; hence, an adjoining street derives its name, now corrupted into *Blubber-lane*. In one of the apartments Richard rested that night. The room seems to have been once elegant, though now in disuse. He brought his own bed-stead, of wood, large and in some places gilt. It continued there 200 years after he left the place, and its remains are now in the possession of Alderman Drake. It had a wooden bottom, and under that a false one, of the same materials, like a floor, and its under ceiling. Between these two bottoms was concealed, a quantity of gold coin, worth about 300 *l.* of our present money, but then worth many times that sum. Thus he personally watched his treasure, and slept on his military chest. Throsby tell us "this inn was kept in the reign of queen Elizabeth, by one Clarke, whose wife hastily making the bed, a piece of gold dropt out, which led to a discovery of the rest; some, the king's own coin. Clerk suddenly grew rich with the spoils of Richard, became mayor of the town, and, at his death, left a fat and wealthy widow. Her servant maid in 1613, conspiring with her sweetheart, robbed and murdered the mistress, for which they were both brought to justice, and executed." So that Richard's property proved as unfortunate as himself. This room seems to have been the last he ever entered, and the bed, the last in which he slept.

On the 17th he marched out of Leicester, with the same parade he had marched in, expecting to meet his rival at Hinckley. He arrived that night at Elmsthorp, eleven miles. As accommodations could not be found in a village, his officers slept in the church, the usual place for sleeping.

Finding he was too early for Henry, he altered his route; and turning towards the right, marched on the 18th to Stableton, six miles, pitched his camp on some grounds called *the Bradshaws*, and, as a security, cast up a breast-work, 300 yards long, and about 50 behind his camp; which with other operations of great labour, prove his stay could not have been less than three days. The camp consisted of two lines. The situation is admirable; not on a hill, but an eminence, fit for observation or contest; a mile and a half east of Bosworth-Field, and two from the top of Amyon-hill, the scene of action. No enemy could approach unseen.

Henry having rested one day at Lichfield, departed towards Tamworth, about six miles.

Throsby pinx.t

Richard the Third's

House and Bedstead.

Walker sculp.ᵗ

Hungerford and Boucher, two knights, who were ordered to attend Richard, deserted Brakenbury their leader, a little beyond Stoney-Stratford; and taking their route through Daventry, Conventry, Birmingham, and Sutton, joined Richmond's army, in the midway between Lichfield and Tamworth; as did also the next day, Aug. 19, Sir John Savage, Sir Bryan Sandford, Sir Simon Digby, &c.

Savage brought with him a body of troops in white coats and hoods, which is the only uniform mentioned on the side of Richmond. These men, three days after, composed part of Richmond's left, which was commanded by Savage.

There are two ways by which an historian deceives his reader; one is by relating false facts; which, if ignorantly done, is a fault, but if with design, a greater; the other is by misrepresenting true ones. Words are the vehicle by which ideas are conveyed. Every thought should impress the reader, exactly in the same manner it did the writer, if it does not, it is imperfectly conveyed. We are given to understand that "Henry immersed in thought, while marching between Lichfield and Tamworth, lingered behind his people, and it became so dark, he could not discover their footsteps, nor hear the sound of the multitude; but wandered backwards and forwards, and durst not enquire his way, for fear of Richard's scouting parties; and that he afterwards found a little village three miles from Tamworth, where he abode the whole night without daring to 'ask a question.' Here we are taught to believe, that Henry *accompanied* his army, which began its march at the verge of night; for it is not more than two hours walk between the two places, even at Henry's musing pace. But the truth is, he did not depart from Lichfield with his people, nor till the evening. They were arrived at Tamworth long before he set off. What detained him, we are not told, but we may easily believe it was something relating to his interest. Nor were there any scouting parties employed by either. This was known to both. Each had their spies, and were well apprized of each other's movements. Henry knew he was doubly secure, for his own army was between Richard and himself, and the two Stanleys between both; if there was danger, it must arise from the inhabitants of the village being friends to Richard; but this idea vanishes when we consider that his body guards, which were twenty light horse, could easily overpower a village. Entering Wittington common, two miles from Lichfield, the road branches into two parts; here a stranger, better versed in the country than Henry, and less musing, might easily be lost. This must have been the erring spot because there is hardly another in this little journey that would admit of a mistake, and the village at which he slept, if he did sleep, must have been Wittington, about a mile distant, and half one to the left of the road he ought to have pursued; because no other can come within the description.

If Henry was deep in thought lest Lord Stanley, pressed by the interest of his son, durst not join him to augment his army, what must have been his thoughts at Wittington, when that army itself, was in danger of a dissolution! Stanley's junction, which had engrossed his thoughts, was an object of great importance, but this was now lost in a greater. That was now become a small stake, but this was his all. Henry was the soul of the army, which, if taken away, the body must crumble. There was a chance even without Stanley, but none without himself. Consternation seized the officers for the absence of their leader; they endeavoured to conceal their amazement for fear of fatal consequences, but were not able. Henry, sensible of the error committed, and its tendency, did all in his power to repair it, by finding his way to Tamworth, as early as twilight would allow.

No man living knew better than he how to turn untoward events to his advantage. He told his people, "he had stept out of the road with *design* to converse with some gentlemen in his interest." Thus one little falshood strengthened that system which was upon the point of dissolving.

Though he *followed* his army to Tamworth, he *left* it before them; for he set out in a few hours to Atherstone, nine miles, attended as before, by his private guards; which is a farther proof there was no fear of scouting parties.

If he arrived at the end of his journey by day light, which, from the shortness of the way, and from the last night's disappointment, we may easily conclude, he might have a view of the important field of blood, and Richard on the right, forming his camp; the distance is eight or nine miles, the intermediate country is flat, Amyon-hill, approached from Atherstone, has the appearance of a mountain, and the Bradshaws were not obstructed from the sight, by the growth of timber.

This early arrival at Atherstone seems to have been a pre-concerted plan between him and the Stanleys, who all three met at night, Aug. 20, secretly in a little close. Though they were firmly united in one cause, it was from different motives. Lord Stanley hated Richard for the cruel attack he had made, two years before, upon his life, for the murder of his friend Hastings, and the young Princes; but durst not espouse Henry's cause for the danger of his son. The persuasions of a wife he loved, and his own sentiments, combated the tender feelings of a father. Impelled by love and inclination, prevented by parental affection, if he did not serve Richmond he could not rest satisfied, if he did, he would lose his son. The husband, the friend, and the father, the most sacred ties we know, opposed each other even to destruction. Henry, dazzled with ambition, viewed matters in a different light; he felt for no man; a crown was the prize, and high calling, for which he pressed forward, and if he could attain it, no matter by what means. Neither the distress of the father, nor the danger of the son, could affect him. Sir William, a man of great honour, despised Richard's actions, and had a friendship for Henry; to which we may add, a small share of ambition. What passed at this triumvirate council of war, never appeared to the light, but it is plain from succeeding events, it was resolved, "That the Stanleys should seem to avoid him, as if friends to Richard. That Richmond should march directly to the field. That Lord Stanley should keep at a distance on the right, and Sir William on the left. That when the two armies of Richard and Henry were drawn up face to face; Lord Stanley should form, and cover the opening between Richard's left and Richmond's right, and Sir William to the same on the opposite side, but join neither; so that when the four armies were marshalled they would form a hollow square. That while the king and the earl were engaged, the two brothers should stand neuter. That if the Earl could overcome the King," which was probable, for they knew Northumberland, who commanded a large body for Richard, would decline fighting, "they should not interfere; but if Richard proved too powerful, they should run all hazards and assist Henry." This politic measure was to serve as a future subterfuge; for though Richard might be vanquished, he might recover his former power, and they be subjected to punishment. They never thought of an event so unusual as a king falling in battle.

It is scarcely in the power of wisdom to form a more complete scheme, or in that of fortune to make one more prosperous. They did the king more mischief, by suspence, and by destroying his plans, than if they had openly joined Henry.

After these resolutions, which carried the destruction of Richard, the two brothers departed, each to his corps; for Richmond's forces had already entered Atherstone, and were encamped in the meadow, north of the church, from thence denominated *the Royal Meadow*. Henry's head quarters was the Three Tuns, which is the same house and the same Three Tuns at this day. It was then undoubtedly the best Inn in Atherstone; this will give the curious observer an idea of a *Royal Inn*, in the time of Richard the Third, and the gradual progress of improvement, to the reign of George the Third. When he surveys this inn, he will think with me, that Henry slept one night, at least, in the black hole. I have made particular enquiries after the little close, where the whole system of British politics underwent a change, and where the fate of nations was determined; but although this dark, and decisive council-room has undergone no remove, tradition has lost it. By an accident, however, it afterwards appeared to be the *Hall-Close*, something less than two acres, one hundred yards behind the Three Tuns, joining the Coleshill road on the left, through which the canal now passes.

The forces of the two brothers had that day marched towards the field. Lord Stanley seemed to fly to Richard for protection, and took his march through Lindley, Higham, and Stoke, to an eminence one mile beyond, called *Gamble's- Close*; upon the ridge of which, the vestiges of his camp are yet visible. This well chosen spot is about six furlongs behind Richard's, and rather on his left. A small rivulet dignified with the name of *Tweed*, glides through the valley between the two camps, which supplied both with water. I was surprized to find the breast-work behind that of the king, where there appeared no danger, and none in the front, where he might be exposed to Henry. This fortification, therefore, must have been constructed for a guard against Lord Stanley; which proves Richard's strong suspicions of that nobleman.

Sir William took his route through Shenton, approached the field on the west, or opposite side to the king and Lord Stanley, and pitched his camp at the foot of Amyon-hill, half a mile from the summit; the traces are yet to be seen, part in the wood, and part in Hewett's ground. The cunning brothers, while strictly faithful to Henry, seemed closely to attend Richard; and Lord Stanley, who had most to lose, attended the closest. Thus were the four commanders situated on the night of the 20th, Richard encamped two miles east of Amyon-hill, Lord Stanley three quarters of a mile towards his rear, Sir William, at the foot of the hill, on the opposite side, and Henry at Atherstone.

The armies were now too near each other to avoid a battle, *neither* could retreat without the utmost hazard. Henry had very little doubt of Richard's fighting; because his courage had been often tried; he had much at stake, and a superior force. But Richard had some doubt of Henry; because he was wholly inexperienced, bore no character as a soldier, and his power was defective. If he should attempt to continue his route for London, Richard could instantly march his troops towards Hinckley, and attack him on the road. But circumvention had no share in this contest, each seemed to *seek* the other to fight him.

Burton tells us, that his great grandfather, John Hardwick, of Lindley, near Bosworth, a man of very short stature, but active, and courageous, tendered his service to Henry, with some troops of horse, the night he lay at Atherstone, became his guide to the field, advised him in the attack, and how to profit by the sun and the wind. I have conversed with several of his descendants, who seemed to hint, that by John's contrivance, Henry won the battle; but as Henry conferred honours upon many of his assistants, why then was John neglected?

Both armies, the next day, Aug. 21, were fully employed. Richard drew up his men in battalia, with as much ostentation, and as broad a front, as his numbers would allow; to answer the same end as their pompous approach to Leicester. While Henry marched from Atherstone, over Wetherly-bridge, almost to the two mile stone; then turned to the left, along Fen-lane, crossed the little rivulet of Tweed, which divides Bosworth-Field from the meadows, and encamped in the first close on the left, in the *White-moors*, one mile from the top of Amyon-hill, and half one behind Sir William's camp.

An army could scarcely proceed with greater secrecy, or expedition, than Henry's had done. From his landing at Milford-Haven, he had marched through Wales to Shrewsbury, and from thence to Bosworth-Field, in fifteen days. Though no warrior, he knew that delays were dangerous, that marching kept up the *spirit* of a people, though it fatigued the body. He remembered the fate of Buckingham.

Whether the superior talents of Henry, or those of John Hardwick, fixed upon this spot for the camp, is uncertain, but nothing could be better chosen. His left, and rear, were secured by the brook, the right, by a swamp, and Sir William became a guard to his front.

The two armies must have been in view of each other all the day. Here they both rested for that night, a little more than two miles asunder. What midnight horrors rent the soul of Richard, or what angelic visions appeared to comfort Henry, I leave to the poetic talents of a Lancastrian, and shall only observe, that neither of them could court repose on the eve of so momentous a day.

Bosworth Field, everlastingly famous, derives its historical name from Bosworth, a shabby market town on the western borders of Leicestershire, one mile distant. Its real name is *Redmoor Plain*, from the colour of the soil; as the meadows on the west are called *White-moors* for the same reason. It belongs to Sutton-Cheney, an adjacent village on the east. It is rather of an oval form, about two miles long, and one broad, and is nearly in a line between Bosworth and Atherstone. The superficial contents may be fifteen hundred acres, inclosed in a ring fence. Part is waste land, part in grass, and part in tillage. The whole field is uneven. The south end, where Henry approached, is three miles from Bosworth, now a wood of four or five acres, and is bounded by the above rivulet. About thirty yards above the wood is a spring called at this day *King Richard's well*. A small discharge of water flows from the well, directly down the hill, through the wood, into the rivulet, but having no channel cut for its passage, it penetrates through the soil, and forms that morass, which Henry is said to have left on his right. Amyon-hill is nearly in the center of the field, and is by much the highest ground; the summit is two or three hundred yards beyond the well. The hill has a steep descent on every side, but is steepest towards the north, or the Bosworth side, and terminates with a rill, a bog, and a flat, called *Amyon lays*. The field extends a mile farther towards Bosworth, but that part was not the scene of action.

Not one human being resides upon this desolate field, or near it; as if *that* place was studiously avoided which had been the scene of blood. The remains of two wretched mud-walled tenements are upon the very places once covered by the troops, Hewit's and another; but the families are fled, and the buildings in ruin.

To have a clear view of this battle, it will be necessary to expunge from our idea the present appearance of the country, and view it as in 1485. For this purpose we must consider all the adjacent lordships uninclosed; and the whole scene as an open country. We are told by some authors that the two armies approached Bosworth Field with *design*, "as a place meet for two to engage;" but they forget that most places were as meet. Those where Richard and

Stanley were encamped, were better. Their march to the field was not impeded. The ground over which Richard's broken forces retreated to Crown-hill, now full of fences, was then wholly without. Richmond's approach to the field was through an open country, but is now an inclosed lane six miles long. Bosworth Field, which was one piece of uncultivated land, without hedge or timber, is now so altered with both, that nothing remains of its former appearance but the shape of the ground. Henry's camp runs in a straight line, about 300 yards from the brook he had crossed, towards Amyon-hill, sometimes within the wood, and sometimes on the White-moors, according to the zig zag of the fence; which proves, that neither the wood nor the hedge were then in being. This hedge now divides the manors of Sutton and Shenton, but if hedges did not then divide the manors, it is reasonable to suppose they did not divide the interior parts. Stoke was the first lordship inclosed, in about 1584, Shenton in 1646, and Sutton is yet open.

All the authors that ever wrote on this battle, three excepted, are partial to Henry; and partiality, at best, disguises truth. They give him every advantage of person, intellectual powers, valour, and the assistance of providence, when in reality he was not entitled to one half. Some tell us his face shone like an angel's, others, that he succeeded from the pious prayers of his mother; others will not allow his army to consist of 5000 men, and some are inclined to make him beat Richard almost without an army. The tide of sentiment ran only one way, and that in favour of the house of Lancaster. But were I allowed to treat royalty with plainness, Richard was an accomplished rascal, and Henry not one jot better. Which had the greatest right to the crown, is no part of the argument; neither of them had any. Perhaps their chief difference of character consisted in Richard's murdering two men for Henry's one; but as a small counter-balance, Richard had some excellencies, to which the other was a stranger. Though we are left in the dark with regard to Richmond's army, yet, if we consider the numbers that joined him in his march through Wales, under their powerful leaders, Griffith, Morgan, Herbert, ap-Thomas, Blount; and in England, with Hungerford, Boucher, Byron, Savage, Sandford, Digby, Hardwick, and many others; also the 2000 French, and the 2000 brought by Talbot at Newport, his numbers could not have been so few as represented by the Lancastrian writers. The same prejudice which diminished Henry's numbers augmented Richard's. If we attentively survey the camps of the four Generals at

Bosworth Field, the night preceeding the battle, it may throw some light on this dark subject, which has been the contest of ages. Though the camps cannot declare the numbers of each, they seem to declare what proportion they bore to each other. Richard's is by far the most extensive, and with the breast works, covers about eighteen acres. Modern cultivation is a dreadful enemy to antiquity. The husbandman has with great labour, destroyed the extent and uniformity of these camps; I could not help smiling while I conversed with the farmer who resides upon the verge of Richard's, when he repeatedly cursed him from spoiling his land; and I asked him whether the shade of Richard might not with equal propriety curse him from spoiling his camp? Richmond's is the most obliterated; but according to the best observation I could make, it covers six or seven acres. Lord Stanley's proceeds along the summit of an eminence, in two lines, is perhaps four acres; and Sir William's, more compact, and more circular, covers about three, hence we may reasonably suppose, the King brought into the field 12,000 men, Richmond more than seven, Lord Stanley five, and Sir William three.

We are now entering upon one of the most important days in the British annals, Monday the 22d of August, 1485, which answers to our present September 2, a day which terminated the contest between the roses. A stream of English blood had continued to flow for thirty years, occasioned by the sword, and the axe. The royal family, though numerous, was nearly extinct, the nobility almost destroyed, and the nation itself, thinned of inhabitants. There had already been many battles, and some of them very destructive, but this was the only one decisive. Though the united strength of all the parties brought into Bosworth Field, did not exceed 28,000 men, yet there had not been a battle since that of Hastings, 419 years before, of such importance; and, as the importance of Hastings consisted in the fall of Harold, so did that of Bosworth in the fall of Richard. Both the sovereigns were usurpers, and both were conquered, and succeeded by those who had no more right than themselves. The death of Harold was owing to a random shot, that of Richard to a daring spirit, but the result of both was the same, the loss of a kingdom. The crown was not to be disputed, with the utmost acrimony, by two of the ablest politicians that ever wore one; they were both wise, and both crafty; equally ambitious, and equally strangers to probity. Richard was better versed in arms, Henry was better served. Richard was brave, Henry a coward. Richard was about five feet four, rather runted, but only made crooked by his enemies; and wanted six weeks of thirty-three. Henry was twenty-seven, slender, and near five feet nine, with a saturnine countenance, yellow hair, and grey eyes. Richard was a man of the deepest penetration! Perfectly adapted to form, and execute a plan; for he generally carried what another durst not attempt, and yet in him, we have a striking instance of the shortness of human foresight. He little thought, when he was clearing his way to the throne, by murder, he was murdering for Henry! That he was clearing the way for a man, whom, of all men, he most detested; that by cutting off one obstacle, he only opened a prospect for another, and by destroying those who guarded the crown for the Plantagenet family, he paved a road for the Tudor.

Sir Simon Digby, having penetrated into Richard's camp, in the character of a night spy, at the utmost hazard of his life, retuned; and informed Henry, at day-break, that the king was preparing for battle. Richmond's trumpets sounded to arms. From this time till the engagement commenced, was about six hours, from four till ten in the morning.

The first persons who attended the king, were Lovell, the Lord Chamberlain; Catesby, the Attorney-General; and Sir Richard Ratcliffe, all privy councellors, to whom he uttered the ill-bodings of his heart. Issuing from his tent, by twilight, he observed a centinel asleep, and is said to have stabbed him, with this remark, "I found him asleep, and have left him as I found him." Perhaps this was the only person Richard ever put to death, who deserved it.

He left his tents standing, and commanded the troops to rendezvous in Sutton field, about the midway to Amyon-hill. Here he drew up in order of battle; his right extended towards the north end of the field, where he made his oration, from which the place acquired, and still bears the name of *Dicken's-nook*.

Though history and tradition are silent, with regard to Lord Stanley's movements, yet there is not a doubt but he marched, and halted with Richard, as if solely attached to his cause, still keeping a little to the rear of his left, for it was evidently his design to amuse his master till the last moment.

Richmond sent an express to Lord Stanley, requesting his assistance in forming his men, for the earnestly wished to have Stanley with him for fear of a disappointment; but he returned for answer, "that the Earl must form them himself, he would come at a convenient season." He afterwards, however, left his own corps to the care of an officer, and privately assisted for a short time.

Henry, though inferior to Richard in numbers, had more horse. Both armies were drawn up exactly alike, each in two lines; the bowmen in the front, the bill-men in the rear, and the horse formed the wings. The principal officers were in armour, that is, each wore a coat of mail, and a helmet. Every man carried a sword, to which were added, for the cavalry, a spear, and for the infantry, some a bow, some a bill, and some a battle-ax. I am inclined to think Richard had artillery, though this is not mentioned by any author; because it was used in the royal army long before that period; and old *Hewit*, who resided fourscore years upon the spot, where the battle was fought, assured me he had found three or four cannon balls, of a smallish size, in his garden, and pointed to the places; I have also other authority. Richard was dressed in the same suit of armour, of polished steel, in which, fourteen years before, he won the battle of Tewkesbury. We are told he had his crown upon his head. He had. But this is an unfair representation, for we should suppose he wore his crown, as a man wears his hat; whereas, he wore the helmet belonging to the suit, and upon this the crown was fixed, by way of crest; the practice of knighthood.

Richard's front line was commanded by John Howard Duke of Norfolk, a faithful veteran, assisted by his son Thomas Earl of Surry, the second by the King himself. In the right of this line, Henry Earl of Northumberland led a considerable body.

Richmond's front, for want of numbers, was spread very thin, to shew to the greater advantage; and was commanded by John de Vere, Earl of Oxford, a firm adherent to the house of Lancaster, whose father and brother, twenty-four years before, died upon one scaffold, for the same cause. This able commander knew well how to marshall Henry's men, and as well how to fight them. From him are descended the houses of St. Alban's and Townshend. Over the right wing was appointed Sir Gilbert Talbot, who joined Henry at Newport, with the Shrewsbury interest; a man of experience and valour, ancestor to the Earls of Shrewsbury and Talbot. Sir John Savage commanded the left, and proved himself worthy of the command. Henry directed the second line, or rather his uncle the Earl of Pembroke, a person of wisdom and prudence. An officer of reputation of the name of Barnard, said to have been descended from the royal line of Scotland, commanded the French. Henry knew nothing, from experience, of the art of war, neither had he the least relish for it, or wish to attain it.

The two chiefs rode through the ranks, and are said to have addressed their followers in an oratorial harrangue, wherein they plentifully abused each other. But these speeches, like those of the House of Commons, perhaps meet the eye rather mended. We can hardly suppose each could extend his eloquence to a hundred and fifty lines in folio.

"Richard assured his well beloved followers, that he owed the crown to their wisdom, that he had been guided by their council, and had approved himself a just king. That this day would try their affections, that he hoped they would keep by their valour, what they had gained by their prudence; that if they wished to live together like brethren, they must fight like lions. That the devil had entered into the heart of an unknown Welchman, who, aided by a company of beggarly thieves, attempted to rob him of his royal dignity; that Richmond was a Welch milksop, without courage, or experience in martial deeds, totally unfit to command an army; that they had nothing to fear from traitors and runagates. That when they should see his banner displayed, they would dread the divine vengeance for acting against their sovereign, and submit to mercy. That the French were braggers and cowards, had often been vanquished by his ancestors, the Plantagenets, and were more apt to run than to fight; and that he himself would that day triumph either in victory or death."

This speech, as is often the case with speeches, contains some truths, but more falsehoods; it varies much from that delivered by the Duke of Cumberland, at the battle of Culloden, who remarked, "If any man is unwilling to engage, either from sentiment or fear, he shall have free liberty to depart." But had Richard made this declaration, two thirds of his army would have instantly vanished.

The oration was followed by a feeble huzza, after which, the army marched in battalia, to Amyon-hill, where they arrived before Henry. Here then must terminate the last stage of a short and turbulent life. Here the exertion of all his powers, in pursuit of glory, must end, in ignominiously falling in one of the most dreary spots in his whole dominions. He must lose that crown for which he had ardently struggled, had basely obtained, and held dearer than himself. Disrobed of royal ermine, he must be degraded beneath a man, hacked to pieces with the swords of Plebeans, die execrating those he was unable to kill; be exhibited naked to every eye but that of a friend, covered with filth, drenched in the blood of those, who had fallen by his sword, lie undistinguished among rabble, and leave a character which no man would envy. This deplorable end of greatness but ill corresponds with the *Lord's anointed*.

The king's right extended to the declivity of the hill, on the Bosworth side, called Cornhill-fruze, or Amyon-lays, and his left towards King Richard's well.

Henry in armour, with his helmet in his hand, rode among the cavalry, and afterwards mounted a little hill, where he addressed the infantry. He observed, "that if ever the Almighty assisted the innocent, or made virtue triumphant over villainy, they were certain of victory. That nothing could be more laudable than to fight against a murderer, a destroyer of his own blood, an expunger of nobility, a firebrand which consumed the country. That Richard and his guilty followers, had wrongfully disinherited him of his lawful right, and unjustly assumed the title of king. He added, they occupy your estates, cut down your timber, and turn out your families to starve. I doubt not but God will deliver them into our hands, or prick their consciences, and cause them to fly. Many follow the tyrant through fear, and only wait an opportunity to join us, and shew they are our friends. Should we be conquered what mercy can we expect from a man who shewed none to his friends, his brother, his nephews, and his wife? We cannot retreat without destruction. What though our numbers be few; the greater will be our praise if we vanquish, and if we fall, the more glorious our death."

Here we behold two Princes, in disputing for a crown descend below the gentlemen, and vilify each other in the language of two Porters disputing for a truss. Though perhaps, this oration was not much truer than the other, yet Henry, brought up in private life, had much the advantage of Richard, for as he had not formed a character, he could lose none; but Richard, long upon the stage of action, had parted with his, never to recover it.

While Lord Stanley was forming, the King sent Sir Robert Brakenbury with this singular, but dreadful message. "My Lord, the King salutes you, and commands your immediate attendance, with your bands, or by — your son shall instantly die.' About the same time Sir Reginald Bray arrived from Henry, pressing Lord Stanley to join him. He replied to Brakenbury, "if the King stains his honour with the blood of my son, I have more; but why should he suffer, I have not lifted a hand against him; I will come at a convenient time."

Lord Stanley seems to have given up his son for lost; but willing, in the last moments, to exert every effort in his favour, took Bray aside, and ordered him to post back to Richmond, about a mile distant, and press him to advance with all speed, against the royal army. This active measure was intended to employ Richard otherwise than in executions.

Brakenbury having delivered Stanley's answer, Richard exclaimed in anger, "This is a false pretence. He is a traitor, and young Strange shall die," and ordered Catesby to see it instantly done.

While the executioner was preparing the axe, and the block; and the youth, in the near prospect of his awful fate, was taken out of the hands of the tent-keeper, as a victim for execution; Lord Ferrers of Chartley, a man of great honor, and humanity, touched with compassion, ventured to remonstrate to the King, "That whatever were the father's crimes, the son was innocent, and it would be cruel to punish the innocent for the guilty; that it might bring disgrace upon their arms, if any blood was shed that day, except by the sword; that envious tongues had already been too free with his princely character, but this would give them greater scope; that there could be no evil in one day's delay, and then punishment might be inflicted where punishment was due. That Stanley had not yet declared against them, but this rash execution would oblige him. That from a family connexion he might not choose openly to espouse the King's cause, but wait some critical moment, or perhaps wait to declare for the victor; that it was better to keep the matter doubtful than force him to become their enemy; and, should the rebels be victorious, they would doubly retaliate the death of Strange. It can do your cause no service, continued he, to take his life, but may an injury." – Richard, convinced by Ferrers's reasons, ordered the execution to be delayed, and perhaps this was the first order of blood he ever revoked.

The King continued in battalia near the top of the hill, unwilling to lose his advantageous ground, while Henry unfurled his banners, sounded the march of death, and advanced from the meadows below.

We are told by our historians, of "a great marsh, that Henry was obliged to pass, though now drained by cultivation." This is another mistake; there neither is, nor ever was one, or any obstruction, but the rivulet mentioned before, which a man might easily jump over; or perhaps when Henry passed it, he might walk over dry-shod; for at that season of the year, the land springs are low, and we have reason to conclude from three little incidents, that the weather was fair, which would keep them lower. When Richard entered Leicester, five days before, it was after sun-set, which supposes that the sun was *seen* to set. In the morning of the battle, it was said to shine on Henry's back, and in the King's face; and when Richard's body was afterwards found among the slain, it was covered with *dust*. All which indicate a fair season: hence we may reasonably conclude, the current was suspended.

Richard was so accomplished a general, that we can hardly suppose him guilty of an oversight; otherwise he seems to have missed a fair opportunity in not waiting for Henry at Wetherly-bridge, also when he perceived him approach the rivulet, the evening before, he might have advanced and engaged him to great advantage. A good general, if he can avoid it, will not be attacked. Oliver always struck the first blow. To wait damps the courage of the people. Though the ceased to flow, yet the water covering the hollows of the bed; the banks, in some places being two or three feet high; the channel forming a curve, and Henry's army straight line, their ranks for a moment would have been broken; when, having an army within bow-shot of their front, no wonder if confusion had ensued. These thoughts could not escape Richard; but he might consider, his situation would be excellent; that Henry must begin the attack at a great disadvantage, for the Hill was against him. He wished Henry to fight, and if he obstructed his passage, he might decline the action, or might attempt another passage, and cause the King to lose his advantageous ground. Richard's was too excellent a situation to be risked even for a better.

Richmond having passed these difficulties unmolested, slowly marched up the ascent, where the wood now stands, the morass formed by King Richard's well, being on his right, and the sun, not on his back, or his right hand, but between both; the King's troops looking on with their bows bent.

As Henry marched forwards he seemed to drive Sir William before him, for in half an hour he would pass over the camp he had quitted. Sir William advanced to the north of the hill, and took his station near Amyon-lays. – Here, I apprehend the King's artillery played upon the enemy; the balls found in Hewit's garden, corroborate the remark. But I could never learn that any execution ensued; perhaps this kind of warlike implement, not being well understood, made no great figure in military practice.

The two armies drawing near each other, Richard's moved a few paces, and both began the bloody scene with a discharge of arrows. The fear of not being soon enough is apt to cause us to be too soon. Perhaps from too great a distance not much execution was done;

but both continuing to advance, instantly came to a close engagement, sword in hand, and the bow was not much used after. Confusion, tumult, and death was the result. Richmond's people fought with some spirit, knowing they must conquer or die. Their all was at stake; they expected no quarter, for in all the battles between the two roses, the axe and the haltar finished what the sword began. Richard's people fought like men, not hearty in the cause. He was no favourite; they were pressed into his service; Henry's were volunteers. If Richard won the battle, his men could not be gainers, nor much losers if he lost it; they were indifferent, and indifference is seldom crowned with success; some were determined not to fight.

During the dreadful conflict, the Earl of Oxford observing his line rather scattered, because spread for shew, ordered that every man should keep near the standard. This causing his men to unite, astonished the King's forces, who desisted from fighting, in dread of some master-stroke of generalship; but recovering from their fears, they renewed the battle, to which Oxford obliged them by beginning first.

Oxford, by closing his men, had shortened his line, which Norfolk perceiving, extended his left with intent to surround him; at that moment Lord Stanley, from flanking both, now joined the right of Richmond, and faced Richard's left, which prevented destruction, and proved a second astonishment to the royalists. If we detach *design* from *action*, Oxford seems to have taken an imprudent step in closing his ranks, because the King would out-flank him. But he was apprized, no doubt, of the determinations in the little close at Atherstone, and narrowed his front with a view to make way for Stanley.

Norfolk and Oxford, leading the vans, naturally approached other, and though sheltered under their helmets, Norfolk knew Oxford by the device on his ensign, a star with rays, and he knew Norfolk by his silver lion. Here we behold the dire effects of party rage. A man becomes rancorous even against his relations, and sheds that blood which is allied to his own. These brave commanders had lived in friendship, and were of one family, Oxford's mother being a Howard, and first cousin to the Duke. They personally attacked each other with their spears, till they were shivered to pieces, then each drew his sword. Norfolk gave the first blow at Oxford's head, which, sliding down his helmet, glanced on the shoulder, and wounded him in the left arm. Oxford, enraged, returned the blow, and hewed the beaver from Norfolk's helmet, leaving the face bare. Oxford, disdaining to fight a man unguarded, declined the combat, and retreated a few paces, when instantly, an arrow from a distant, and unknown hand, hit the Duke in the face, and pierced the brain –Thus fell John Howard, Duke of Norfolk, one of the fairest characters of the age, notwithstanding his adherence to Richard. He was descended from the Mowbrays, Dukes of Norfolk, and by a daughter of Brotherton, from the Royal line. He was early bred to arms, and had, while Sir John Howard, faithfully served Edward the Fourth, in the Lancastrian quarrel, who raised him to peerage by the the title of Lord Howard; and Richard the Third, in the first of his reign, conferred on him the Dukedom of Norfolk, and on his son the Earldom of Surry, both which his descendants enjoy. He was warned by a bundle of papers left at his gate not to join Richard, and again, by a coarse rhyme upon his tent door, the night preceding the battle

> "Jack of Norfolk be not too bold,
> For Dicken thy master is bought and sold;"

but he had taken an oath to Richard, and he could not recede. He revered the *King*, but lamented the errors of the *man*. – Oxford, though an enemy, felt for his fall, and declared, "A better knight could not die, though he might in a better cause."

Surry had already acted the hero, but his father's death inspired him with such revenge, that he laid several at his feet; he followed his blow as if determined his single sword should win the field; when approaching Talbot, they furiously engaged. Talbot was provoked that a veteran, like himself, could not overcome a stripling almost in his first appearance in arms. Some of his followers surrounded young Surry, with a design to take him alive, but he resolved not to yield, but die, as his father had just done, sword in hand. Here an affecting spectacle offers, two worthy characters, Norfolk and Surry, the first stretched a victim at the feet of his son, and the son oppressed by those who had caused the death of his father, without one friend to support him. he fought in the midst of numbers till his strength was exhausted, when two of the King's courageous knights, Sir Richard Clarendon, and Sir William Conyers, were resolved to rescue him or perish in the attempt. This Savage observing, who himself as well as his sword, was dyed in blood, surrounded them with some of his people, who cut them to pieces. Savage made any attempts to save them, but could not; and now, Surry was again left alone to cope with a surrounding multitude, and his powers gone. This being remarked, a second attempt was made, by a private soldier to take him prisoner, which Surry disdaining, collected strength from anger, and at one desperate blow, cut off his arm, which fell to the ground. This done, he presented the hilt of his sword to Talbot, desiring him to put a period to his life, that it might not be taken by an ignoble hand. "God forbid, says the generous Talbot, that I should stain my character with the blood of so brave a youth. You have not erred; the fault was your father's." "I wonder, replied Surry, that the noble Talbot should insult the vanquished, in distress. We had the right, but the sword is transferring it to you. I shall never repent the choice I made, neither can my honour suffer by that choice. Our maxim is *To support the Crown of England*. Whoever wears it, I will fight for; nay, were it placed upon a hedge-stake, I should think it my duty to defend it." This expression was afterwards reported to Henry; and though Surry was sent to the Tower, it proved a means of reconciliation, and he afterwards fulfilled his own remark, by becoming a faithful adherent to Henry. This Earl of Surry may be said to have *produced a House of Lords*, for from him descended eleven distinct families of the name of *Howard*, who rose into Peerage, by the titles of Norfolk, Nottingham, Bindon, Northampton, Eskrick, Norwich, Suffolk, Berkshire, Carlisle, Stafford, and Effingham; a similar case of fertile nobility is not upon record.

It was now past eleven. The battle had continued about one hour, without much advantage gained by either side, except, that Richard had lost Norfolk and Surry, his principal officers. No part of their forces had been vanquished. Only the front line of each army had been engaged, nor had they much varied their ground. The two chiefs had kept their station, Richard in the center of his rear, and Henry, towards the left of his; when Richard, attended by his officers, making an effort to assist the van, a scout came upon the full run, and informed the King, "that Richmond was posted behind the hill, with a slender attendance." Richard, fired at the news, altered his design of reinforcing the van, and marching up the ascent, the person of Henry was particularly pointed out to him, for he did not know him. He grasped his spear, fixed it in the rest, and exclaimed, "Let all true Knights attend me, and I will soon put an end to the quarrel; but if none will follow, I will try the cause alone."

After such a declaration, it would have been difficult even for a coward to stay behind. He instantly spurred his horse into a gallop, and rode out of the right flank, attended, among others, by Francis Lord Viscount Lovell, Walter Lord Ferrers, Sir Richard Radcliffe, Sir Gervis Clifton, Sir Robert Brakenbury, Sir William Catesby, &c. with their followers; none of them shewing signs of fear, except Catesby. They rode directly towards Henry, with the King in front, and Sir William Stanley with 3,000 men standing neuter at his right elbow. It is a melancholy reflection, but was happily hid from their eyes, that every one of them, Lovell excepted, was following his Sovereign to death!

Richard is represented as having lost the battle, and disdaining to survive the disgrace, rushed into the heat of the action, to sell his life at the dearest rate. Here seems another mistake; for his desperate plan, formed in a moment, was not an ill-concerted one; he was still uncertain whether Stanley would declare for Henry, and as Henry was thinly guarded, he stood a fair chance, by a bold stroke, of being instantly dispatched, and then the field was won. Besides, Richard's courage was invincible, ten such men might have withstood a hundred. This was one of those daring enterprizes, which is condemned or applauded, according to its good or ill success. By the last sentence in his oration, he seemed resolved to embrace an opening, should one offer, however dangerous.

Though Richard took his spear, he did not use it, but trusted to his sword. Sir William Brandon, the Earl's standard bearer, was the first person he approached, who, fascinated as with a basilisk, at the intrepid boldness of the King, could neither resist nor depart, but seemed to fall by his own astonishment. Richard at one stroke, cleft his head, seized the standard, and with a vengeance threw it on the ground. This was a red dragon, upon a green and white silk, the ensign of Cadwallador, the last king of the Britons, maternal ancestor to Henry.

He instantly attacked the powerful Sir John Cheney, who, after the faint resistance of a moment, was unhorsed. These were not the acts of a little, puny, decrepit fellow, with a withered arm! He paid no attention to those on the right, or the left, except to kill them, but the spirit of the hero growing into that of the mad-man, he thought of nothing but cutting his way to Henry.

If Henry moved at all it was backwards. He continually permitted his people to interfere, suffered their numbers to thicken, and never shewed the least sign of advancing. The ferocity of Richard would have terrified a better man than Henry.

Hitherto Richard's was a well laid plan; he was winning a battle by consternation on one side, and valour on the other. All sides gave way; Richmond was in the utmost danger, and fortune seemed much inclined in the King's favour. Sir William Stanley observing this, instantly closed with his 3,000 men, nearly surrounded those with the King, prevented others from advancing, who shewed no great inclination to advance, and by dint of numbers, and surprize, gave an effectual turn to the fortune of the day. This was perhaps the most critical moment in Richard's life. Victory had suspended the scales between the combatants, which were as equally poized as with a level guinea. Richard's seemed at length to preponderate. She beheld it with a smile; but instantly turned away, Stanley threw is whole weight into Henry's scale, and the King's was found waiting. Had Sir William deferred his assistance but one minute, he might have deferred it for ever; Henry must either have fallen or fled.

Here we stand amazed at two similar incidents, which happened nearly together, to which history cannot add a third. The Duke of Buckingham, as mentioned before, was the person who set the crown upon Richard's head, and Richard, in return, cut off Buckingham's. Thus a favour too great to be rewarded with benefits, is rewarded with death. Sir William, by this timely support, was the person who alone set the crown on Henry's head, nay, perhaps, saved his life; and yet Henry, ten years after, beheaded Sir William. One would think, if a man confers a remarkable favour, it ought to be on him who has no *powers* of return, for fear of incurring the greatest injury. The only crime *openly* alledged against this unhappy man was, that while Perkin Warbeck obtruded himself upon the world, for the Duke of York, he should say, "If I was sure he was the son of Edward the Fourth, I would never draw my sword against him." A man may be charged with treason for *fighting*, but we rarely find him so charged for declaring he will not. Henry was fond of seeing the officers of the crown grow rich by lucrative places, and as fond of quarrelling with them, that he might draw those riches to himself. Thus he filled the places, and reaped the profits. Stanley loved money, was immensely rich, and his greatest crime was thought to be his wealth. Henry must have been a complete master of address, or he durst not have ventured to pay a friendly visit to Lord Stanley immediately after he had destroyed his brother.

The eye of fear is ever watchful. Catesby was the first who saw the approach of Stanley, apprized the King of his danger, and assured him there was no disgrace, when destruction was at hand, in consulting his safety by flight; and instantly retreated. Richard, with an angry look, branded him for a coward, and declared that he himself would never submit.

During this dreadful conflict it was the fortune of Brakenbury, and Hungerford to meet. Brakenbury called him traitor, and accused him in the harshest terms for deserting his Sovereign, to serve a rebel, and an out-law. Hungerford replied, "He would return him something more solid than words," and aimed so violent a blow at his head, silvered with grey hairs, as would have pierced his burganet, had not Brakenbury that moment raised his left arm to sustain it; but the violence of the stroke slit his shield, and rendered it useless. Hungerford delivered his own target to his squire, saying at the same time to Brakenbury, "He would take no advantage of a naked antagonist, they should now fight on equal terms." But it may be replied, though they were equal in arms, they were not equal in years, for it was active life against old age. They renewed the conflict, aiming many furious blows at each other's head, till Brakenbury's helmet was knocked to pieces, and himself sorely wounded. Boucher called out, "brave Hungerford, spare his life, he has been our friend, and may be so again?" but it was too late, his wounds were mortal, and he breathed his last on the ground. He was a gentleman of strict honour, and would not condescend to stain his hands with the blood of the young Princes, though perhaps tempted by his Sovereign.

Should a tyrant arise, who invades the rights of mankind, it would be prudent for every man to rise against him, because all are interested; for the injustice he offers to one, he would to another. But when two worthless characters, like those of Richard and Henry, contend for that which neither have a right to, what pity it is they are not left personally to decide the dispute, without drawing in the innocent, nay, even fathers, brothers, and friends to destroy each other. Sir John Byron, and Sir Gervis Clifton, were intimate friends, and neighbours, being both Nottinghamshire Gentlemen. And though Byron fought under Henry, and Clifton under Richard, it no way diminished their friendship, but proved, what rarely happens, that friendship genuine. They had exchanged a prior oath, "that if either of them was vanquished, the other should intercede with the conqueror, that the estate of the loser might not be forfeited, but enjoyed by his family." While Clifton was bravely fighting in the troop, he received a blow which overpowered him, and he fell. Byron observing the fall, quitted the ranks, and ran to the relief of his suffering friend, sustained him on the ground, guarded him with his shield, and intreated him to surrender. Clifton replied, "All is over; I beg my dear friend you will remember the oath between us. Victory is your's. Use all your interest, that my lands may not be taken from my children." The worthy Byron, upon the point of renewing his promise, perceived his friend was departing, and exclaimed with emotion, "Stay, my dear Clifton, stay!" but alas! the wound was mortal, and the unfortunate Clifton expired in the field. Perhaps Byron performed the oath he took, and the promise he would have renewed; for Sir Gervis Clifton, the descendant of him who fell, now enjoys the same estate, which was possessed by his ancestors many centuries prior to the Battle of Bosworth. The quarrel between the two roses was peculiarly unfortunate to the Clifton family, for though this gentleman fell for the house of York, his father, fourteen years before, being vanquished at Tewkesbury, in fighting for that of Lancaster, was one of sixteen officers who took sanctuary in the church. Edward the Fourth pursued them with a drawn sword, but was met in the porch, by the priest, who, presenting the sacrament, would not suffer him to defile the place with blood, nor even enter till he had promised a pardon. A striking instance of ecclesiastical power. This was on Saturday the fourth of May, but by Monday, Edward had forgot his promise, and brought every one of them to the block.

Richard might now be said to have been in the midst of a fire, and that of his own kindling. He continued his ferocity till his powers and his friends failing, for every one of his followers was either fallen or fled, he stood single in the center of his enemies; when, becoming less desperate, through weakness, many durst approach within the length of sword, who, some minutes before, durst not venture within the length of a spear. Richmond's people having so fair a mark as a hated King, unguarded, were eager to kill Richard; and Richard, dreadfully circumstanced, had no objection to be killed. Despicable as his body is represented, he sustained a great deal of beating, before he was beaten down; but as the sturdiest oak must give way to a multitude of axes, Richard at length fell, fighting an army! His body was covered with wounds. His helmet, which, like a cullendar, was full of holes, had lost the crown, and was beaten into every form but the right. Had a stranger afterwards examined the field, the most abused helmet he could find, he might safely conclude had been Richard's.

Thus fell Richard the Third, one of the greatest heroes, and one of the most dishonest men recorded in history. Perhaps he was the last man slain in this battle, except in the pursuit, and if so, the last in the Plantagenet quarrel. The contest had continued more than thirty years, in which had been killed 100,000 men, but what is rather singular, the first man that fell, and the last, stood at the head of the house of York, Richard, Earl of Cambridge, and his grandson Richard the Third.

While we survey this awful field, the first in consequence in the whole island, that of Battle in Sussex excepted, we consider it as classic ground. Here contemplation brings in review, important deeds, and their more important effects. To this field, Richard brought an aching heart, and a faithless army, lost both, and was declared a traitor, because unfortunate. Richmond approached it, doubtful whether he should find a throne, or a block; whether he should put on the ermine, or the shrowd. Here Norfolk fell, out of gratitude to that prince, who had raised him to greatness; and the brave Surry was within a hair's breadth of losing that life, which replenished both houses of Parliament. Here Brandon sunk under Richard's sword, and his own surprize; and Sir William Stanley set the crown on Henry's head, by which he lost his own. Oxford, from a desolate wanderer, recovered the ancient patrimony of his house, and Lord Stanley, while betraying his master, could have nothing in view, but victory, or the axe; nay, destruction hung over the Stanley family, by a slender thread. On this spot Richard owed his ruin to his valour, and that valour prevented the ruin of the Stanleys. Here a friendship was displayed between Byron and Clifton, which is no where surpassed in history. Here Conyers and Clarendon suffered for the most generous act, and here the fate of a mighty nation was determined.

From the time Richard galloped out of the right flank, till he fell, could not be more than fifteen minutes, but they were some of the most remarkable minutes we read of. They for ever closed the bleeding wounds of the two houses. They extinguished the ancient and heroic line of Plantagenet. A period was put to the enormous power of the Barons, which had bound the people, and bullied the crown; and to the still more enormous power of the priesthood, which had bullied both. They dispelled the clouds of ignorance and superstition, and obliged the witch, the ghost, and the wizard for ever to hide their faces. They opened the door for light, knowledge, and letters. They were the dawn of the arts. The world was taught to consider the lower ranks of men as part of the human species, who, before had only been considered as slaves and villains; that every man had a right to his property, and if he possessed no property, he had still a right to himself. They promoted a beneficial union between England and Scotland; which, being founded on natural principles, became permanent, by which harmony is preserved, and the lives of thousands saved. The united kingdom was taught by these fifteen minutes, to increase in commerce, in riches, in civilization, in power, and soon to rise the arbitress of Europe. If we consider the part of the field where Richmond marched up, with the morass on his right: his own situation, towards the left of the second line, the hill over which the King marched, when the first saw him, and the way the royal forces retreated, they will nearly point out the situation of both armies and the spot where Richard fell. This spot must have been at the foot of the hill, near Amyon-lays; and the united traditions of the country serve to prove it. They report, that Richard was slain while his horse was set fast in a bog. Sir William's people certainly surrounded him; and while in that situation, they must have fought upon firm ground. But when the King was left alone, by losing his friends, he was probably driven into the bog, formed by the springs, and the rivulet, where he fell.

The blood of the slain tinged the little stream long after the battle, particularly in rain. The battle being fought in a dry season, much of the blood would lodge upon the ground, become baked with the sun, and the longer in washing off; which inspired a belief in the country people, that the rivulet runs blood to this day, and they frequently examine it. Possessed with this opinion, they refuse to drink it; while King Richard's well, on the other side of the hill, has had, by the nymphs and the swains, many an hogshead of sugar dissolved in its water. Thus the honourable blood of the Plantagenets, the pride of English history, which had swayed the British sceptre for ages, was mixed with that of the peasant, and both went to supply a gutter.

At the death of the King, opposition ceased, part of his troops remained in the field, the rest fled different ways, but chiefly towards Stoke, leaving Sutton-Cheney, and Dicken's-nook, near a mile on the left, and were pursued with slaughter, by the victors. This is corroborated by the human bones and war-like implements often found, particularly in about 1585, when the lordship of Stoke was inclosed; and by the pits, or hollows, with which, their route to crown hill is marked; for though tradition can assign no reason for the hollows, I judge they were the graves of those who fell, and were promiscuously tumbled in by heaps, which would sink into hollows, as the bodies decayed.

Authors differ exceedingly with regard to the slain, and I am not able to set them right. But as only the front lines were engaged, and as neither side shifted their ground, nor fought with remarkable vigour, I am inclined to think the numbers which fell during the battle, were nearly equal; and as Henry is said to have lost about one hundred, Richard, perhaps did not lose many more. The greatest carnage must have been in the pursuit, which continued two miles, and about forty or fifty minutes. This would probably increase the number to nine hundred. Henry attended his people in this species of destruction; Lord Stanley pursued the vanquished troops, and Sir William staid to pillage the field.

We are told, the greater part of Richard's army never struck a blow; that is, the two wings, and the rear; which proves they were not firm to his interest; how then could he prepare a sufficient force to oppose the two Stanleys! He could not be said even to command his own army! Part of these neutral forces, which composed the rear, were under the command of Henry Earl of Northumberland, amounting to two or three thousand men, who grounded their arms, to shew Richmond's people, they had nothing to fear from *them*. The keen-eyed Richard had before expressed to Lord Ferrers, his suspicions of Northumberland, and, perhaps for that reason, placed him in the rear to watch him himself; the honest Ferrers, like many a duped person after him, "wondered there could be such duplicity in the world," forgetting that he who talks most of his probity has none. At the same time Ferrers renewed his promises of fidelity, for which he received his sovereign's applause and his thanks. Northumberland had but little reason to be satisfied with the house of York; perhaps he had not forgot the death of his father, in the cause of Lancaster, at Towton-field, when that blood-thirsty butcher, Edward the Fourth, ordered his troops to give no quarter. There thirty-six thousand innocent people were slaughtered, in disputing which of two men should wear a crown, claimed by both, but deserved by neither. Nor was it of the least consequence to the multitude, which wore it. Probably the prior warning given to the Duke of Norfolk, by the papers left at his gate, and the distich over his tent door, the night preceding the battle, originated from Northumberland. He experienced Henry's smiles, was instantly taken into favour, honoured with a seat at the council-board, proved faithful to his interest, and four years after lost his life in his service.

Richard was the only English monarch since the conquest, who fell in battle, and the second who fought in his crown; an indication of courage, because from such a distinguishing mark, the person of majesty is readily singled out for destruction; Henry the Fifth appeared in his at Agincourt, which was the means of *saving* his life, by sustaining a stroke with a battle-axe, which cleft it. But Richard's falling off, in his last fiery struggle, was taken up by a private soldier, who contrived to secret it in a bush in the field, perhaps with a view to secure it for himself. But being discovered, it was delivered to Sir Reginald Bray; hence arises the device of a crown in a hawthorn bush, at each end of Henry's tomb, in Westminster Abbey.

When the pursuit was over, Bray delivered the battered crown to Lord Stanley, who placed it on Henry's head, hailed him King, and, as usual, sung Te-Deum, and taught the soldiers to huzza the rural monarch with, "Long live King Henry." This was performed upon a hill near Stoke, from thence called crown-hill, forty-three acres. At the inclosure of the manor, this hill was divided into four parts, three of which bear the names of upper, middle, and lower *Crown-hill*, and the fourth *Hollow-meadow*, from the soldiers hollaing when Henry was crowned. Tradition tells us, they raised their voices to the highest pitch, to inform their companions in Bosworth-field, in full view of each other across the valley, that the pusuit was over, and the victory compleat. Thus Henry acquired with ease what he valued the most, and had the longest wished for, *a crown*. It is curious to observe what prudence and perseverence he used to overthrow the house of York, and acquire it. Our historians erroneously suppose, the two years between the defeat of Buckingham and the victory of Bosworth, were spent at the court of France; but great part of that time was employed in travelling secretly among the powerful families in Wales, to solicit their aid, and some little, in paying his addresses to Miss Herbert. Pennant in his tour tells us that while Henry was at Tremostyn in Flintshire, about dinner-time, a party attached to Richard, arrived with intent to apprehend him, but, with the assistance of the family, he had just time to leap out of a back window and escape through a hole, which to this day is called *the King's hole*. Richard-ap-Howel, lord of the place, paternal ancestor to the present Sir Roger Mostyn, afterwards attended him to Bosworth-field. When the battle was over, Henry invited him to court, but the honest Welchman nobly replied, *I will dwell among mine own people*. Henry then presented him with the sword and belt he had worn that day, with which, attended by his followers, he retreated into Wales, the little king of half a country; and these relicks of victory were, till lately, preserved in the family. There is but one instance upon record, where a crown has been won with less difficulty, that of the revolution between James the Second, and William the Third; the reason of both was the same, a national dislike to the reigning prince; both may be said to have been reduced by their own forces. Henry was the only sovereign we read of, crowned in the open field, and his military coronation was performed without a prayer.

The track which Richmond marched from the camp to the engagement, and from thence to Crown-hill, formed the letter V reversed, Λ he approached by the left limb, and retreated by the right. The road by which the King's troops advanced, and retreated forms the same, and as both retreated one way, they unitedly form something like a double u, M.

This battle, destructive to many, furnished the country people with domestic utensils. A blacksmith assured me he had found a sword blade, which he used for a drill-bow. An old woman converted part of another into a hanging spit, for roast-meat, so that it continued its ancient practice of wounding flesh. Between King Richard's well, and the summit of Amyon-hill, is a bed of sand, perhaps an acre, the only one in the whole neighbourhood; a gentleman told me he saw dug out of this bed, a sword and a candlestick, a yard beneath the surface, both perfect. The sword no doubt was a genuine antique, but the candlestick was probably the relic of a thief, who had stolen sand in the night.

An antiquary of my acquaintance, travelling over these solitary regions, bought a sword of a peasant, for six-pence, found in opening a gravel pit, near Stoke, in high preservation; but as it carried no ancient marks, its authenticity was doubtful. I therefore applied to every sword-maker in Birmingham, who all agreed, it was of German construction, and by comparing it with others of various periods, left no reason to doubt its being the spoils of Bosworth Field, and had been drawn by an officer of horse. The ignorance of the seller, and the miserable price it sold for, prove there was no deceit in the bargain; they also prove the great value of money, and the small value set by the natives, upon a leading curiosity, which if made public, would readily have brought five guineas.

Henry was not the only person who received honours in the field, for the knighted several gentlemen, as Gilbert Talbot, John Mortimer, Richard-ap-Thomas, Robert Points, Humphry Stanley, John Turberville, Robert Willoughby, Hugh Pershull, Richard Edgcombe, John Bickenyle, De Baron de Carow, &c.

Crown-hill, prosperous to Henry, and his followers, being upon sale some years back; a gentleman, perhaps from the singularity of the place and the actions upon it, wished to become the purchaser. The price was eleven hundred pounds. Having no money, he hired the whole sum at five per cent. Suffering the interest to run in arrears, the mortgagee obliged him to sell the estate, to discharge the debt. This happening under Lord North's administration, when the American contest had reduced the value of land, it brought only nine hundred, which left a large debt uncovered. To secure this, he was obliged to mortgage, to the same person, a paternal estate of about one hundred acres, situate between Crown-hill, and Lord Stanley's camp. A second neglect of interest, and a repeated renewal of the mortgage, soon devoured the paternal estate, which was sold in Nov. 1787, to clear the original debt of Crown-hill. Thus, upon that spot where Henry found a crown, and his adherents victory, and honour, another found his ruin.

Sir William Brandon was the only person of note, who fell on the side of Henry; but the officers on that of Richard suffered greatly, among whom were John Duke of Norfolk, Walter Lord Ferrers, Sir Richard Radcliffe, Sir William Conyers, Sir Richard Clarendon, Sir Robert Brakenbury, the Lord Zouch, and Sir Jervis Clifton. Lord Lovell ran away, and two years after fought against Henry, at Stoke, where he lost his life, or at least was heard of no more. Humphry, and Thomas Stafford, took sanctuary in St. John's, Gloucester. The grandmother of the Lord Ferrers slain here, was heiress of the house of Birmingham. He himself was ancestor to the present Lord Hereford, and by marrying the heiress of Ferrers, was the first proprietor of Castle-Bromwich of the name of Devereux. His great grandson erected the present hall, in the reign of Queen Elizabeth.

The body of King Richard being found among the slain, covered with wounds, dust, and blood, after suffering many shameful indignities, was hung over a horse, like a calf, behind a pursuivant at arms, named *Blanch Sanglier*, or White-boar, the name of his office, he wearing a silver boar upon his coat, the cognizance of Richard, and was carried to Leicester in triumph, that afternoon. The corpse was perfectly naked, the feet hung on the side, the hands on the other, and the head lately adorned with a crown, dangling like a thrum-mop. No King ever made so degraded a spectacle; humanity and decency ought not to have suffered it. *Carte* says they tied a rope about his neck, which is very probable, and perhaps about his feet, or he could not well have been sastened to the horse. this was meant as a disgrace to Richard, but it reflected more upon Henry, ot his followers; for to insult weakness is highly blameable, but more to insult the dead.

The corpse was exposed two days to public view, in the town hall; this was Henry's policy, to prevent a future imposter, and his pride to shew himself a conqueror, and then interred without ceremony, in the Gray-friers' church. Here Richard rested about fifty years, with a scrubby alabaster monument erected over him by Henry. At the destruction of religious houses, his remains were turned out of their little tenement by the town's people, and lost, and his coffin of stone, was converted into a watering-through at the White-Horse, in Gallow-tree-gate. Thus all the grandeur for which Richard exerted uncommon talents, ended in a stile below a beggar.

I took a journey to Leicester, in 1758, to see a trough which had been the repository of one of the most singular bodies that ever existed, but found it had not withstood the ravages of time. The best intelligence I could obtain was, that it was destroyed about the latter end of the reign of George the First, and some of the pieces placed as steps in a cellar, at the same inn where it had served as a trough.

All Richard's credits expired with him, the breath of the Tudors compleatly blasted his character; even the country people, to this day, seldom honour him with his real name, but depreciate him with the epithet of *King Dick*.

The fluctuations of the human mind are remarkable; the tide of applause runs parallel with the tide of prosperity; when this falls, the voice of popular favour falls with it. While the house of York swayed the British sceptre, the *white rose* was held in repute, bloomed on the bosom of beauty, and on the sign-post of the publican; but when that house fell, it faded with it, and from that moment was elevated no more. Even now, if ever we see the sign of the rose, it is always a red; nay, it was but recently, that this innocent and lovely flower recovered its prestine credit; for in the contests between the houses of Stuart and Brunswick, it was supposed to be tainted with the smell of treason.

During the sovereignty of Richard, the *White-Boar* also was a common sign. A compliment was paid him without the house, and his health drank within; but at his death, the landlords took down their White-Boars, and where any one omitted it, the fickle multitude pulled it down for him; and to this day, we often behold the sign of the *Black Boar*, and the *Blue-Boar*, but never the white. Tradition tells us, the Inn where Richard slept at Leicester, was the White-Boar, in honour of the sovereign, but the proprietor, like others, was obliged to change it for the blue. The King had also added to the college of Heralds, a pursuivant at arms called Blanch-Sanglier, or White-Boar, from his own crest, mentioned above, as former princes had created *Blue-Mantle, Rouge-Cross, &c.* but after this officer had been obliged, in a scandalous manner, to carry his dead sovereign, Henry annihilated the office, and substituted that of *Rouge-Dragon* in honour to himself.

The sagacious Henry instantly dispatched Sir Robert Willoughby from Leicester to Sheriff-Hutton, in Yorkshire, to seize one of the greatest, and most unfortunate of the human race, Edward Earl of Warwick, only son of George Duke of Clarence, the last of the Plantagenet race, whose melancholy story can scarcely be read without tears. In him we behold the highest degree of innocence, and of punishment. The blood of this inoffensive prince, has left a stain upon Henry's character, which nothing can efface.

Although Catesby, through whose treachery Hastings lost his life, endeavoured to save his own by deserting Richard in his last moments, yet he was taken prisoner, carried with others, in triumph to Leicester, and some say, executed that day, others the next, but all are mistaken; for Henry staid two days at Leicester, and then pursued his course to London, where he arrived on Sunday the 28th, carrying in front Richard's three standards, the chief of which was St. George; these he erected in Paul's church, and left Catesby for execution. The last will of this victim to conquest, which is curious, and may be seen in Dugdale's Warwickshire 552, proves him alive the 25th, three days after the battle. It also proves him, under his own hand, a dishonest man, in amassing a fortune by unfair means. He expresses a friendship for Lovell, and seems angry with Stanley and Strange. He was descended from a very ancient family at Lapworth, near Birmingham, was bred to the law, in which profession he had acted for Buckingham, Hastings, and the Stanleys. Two gentlemen from the north, of the name of Brecher, were beheaded with him. Thus the first regal act performed by

Henry, was an act of tyranny, the very fault for which his predecessor was desposed.

That Richard was not so little beloved as our historians represent, appears by the veneration in which he was held, long after his death, in the northern countries, where he resided in youth; also by the following gentlemen, who were firm in his interest, and were all at the battle, for which they were attainted by Henry when he called a parliament: John Duke of Norfolk, Thomas Earl of Surry, Francis Lord Lovell, Walter Lord Ferrers, John Lord Zouch, Robert Harrington, Richard Charlton, Richard Ratcliffe, William Barkley, of Weley-castle, near Birmingham, Robert Middleton, James Harrington, Robert Brakenbury, Thomas Pilkington, Walter Hopton, William Catesby, Roger Wake, William Sapcoat, of Huntingdonshire, Humphry Stafford, William Clarke, of Wenlock, Jeffrey St. German, Richard Wilkins, Herald at Arms, Richard Revell, of Derbyshire, Thomas Poulter, of Kent, John Welch, otherwise Hastings, John Kendall, Secretary to King Richard, John Buck, related to the historian, Andrew Rat and William Brampton, of Burford.

Sir Gervis Clifton, not being in this catalogue of unfortunate names, is a farther evidence that the faithful Byron fulfilled his friendly engagement.

As the battle of Bosworth was the last between the roses, I shall exhibit a dreadful table of those scenes of butchery, which originated from ambition, and are shocking to humanity [*see following pages*].

No.	Battles.	When fought.	Commanders for York.
1	St. Alban's	May 23, 1455	Duke of York
2	Blore heath	Sep. 23, 1459	Earl of Salisbury
3	Northampton	July 10, 1460	Earl of Warwick
4	Wakefield	Dec. 31, 1460	Duke of York
5	Mortimer's cross	Feb. 2, 1461	Earl of March
6	St. Alban's	Feb. 17, 1461	Earl of Warwick
7	Towton-field	Mar. 29, 1461	Edw. the Fourth
8	Hexham	June 24, 1463	Mar. of Montague
9	Banbury	July 26, 1469	Earl of Pembroke
10	Stamford	April 27, 1470	Edw. the Fourth
11	Barnet	April 14, 1471	Edw. the Fourth
12	Tewkesbury	May 4, 1471	Edw. the Fourth
13	Bosworth	Aug. 22, 1485	Richard the Third

Commanders for Lancaster.	Who victorious.	Slain.
Duke of Sumerset	York	5,600
Lord Audley	York	2,400
Duke of Sumerset	York	14,000
Queen Margret	Lancaster	2,200
Earl of Pembroke	York	4,800
Queen Margret	Lancaster	2,900
Duke of Sumerset	York	36,776
Duke of Sumerset	York	2,100
Sir John Conyers	Lancaster	6,500
Sir Robert Wells	York	13,000
Earl of Warwick	York	10,000
Duke of Sumerset	York	4,000
Earl of Richmond	Lancaster	900
		105,176

It must be observed, the numbers specified to have been slain in some of the battles, were such *only* who fell on the losing side; nor were those included who suffered in cold blood, by the axe, and the halter, therefore the numbers destroyed in this civil contest must have far exceeded 105,000.

Henry wished to shew to the world he had a better claim to a crown than those derived from marriage, parliament, or the house of Lancaster, by being descended from an illustrious line of kings, even from the first prince that ever swayed a British sceptre. Possessed of a true Welch genealogical spirit, he instituted a commission of antiquaries, to trace his pedigree. The complaisant commissioners endeavoured to gratify his pride by opening the ancient sluices of royal blood, and infusing a copious stream into his veins. After rising to his grandfather, Owen Tudor, who married Queen Catherine, they were contented with three generations of gentlemen; when supposing they had lost sight of detection, they verged upon nobility. They then laid hold upon one one of the fifteen tribes of North Wales; and though they afterwards sunk his ancestors into private life, for eleven generations, they passed in the next through an Earl of Dunstable. A few more removes brought them to Prince Arthur, and another few, to a King *Coel Godeboe* amounting to thirty one removes above Henry; and though again they let his ancestors sink into subjects, during fourteen generations more, they seized upon the famous *Belin*, who lived seventy years before Christ, and pronounced him the forty-fifth from Henry. We then open upon a sumptuous race of Kings, in regular ascent for forty-one generations! So numerous a progeny of royal ap's is wholly unknown in the history of man, and would stagger even the faith of a Chinese chronologer. This brigs us to the celebrated *King Lear*. And now we have but nine steps to mount till we arrive at *Brutus*, fondly supposed the first inhabitant of this island. Thus Henry's pride feasted upon the froth of antiquity, and his wisdom was duped by his vanity. I am surprized the modest commissioners stopt short at Brutus, for I have seen the cobweb ladder of a Welch pedigree stretched up to Adam, and the author, even then, seemed disappointed he could rear it no higher, but perhaps they were not able to marshall another troop of Kings.

CHARACTER *of the* KING

Richard the Third, of all the English Monarchs, bears the greatest contrariety of character. One would think, that period obscured in darkness, which admits of such flagrant contradictions, and yet, the bold lines of the time, are clearly seen, and easily described.

Some few have conferred upon him almost angelic excellence, have clouded his errors, and blazened every virtue that could adorn a man. Others, as if only extremes could prevail, present him in the blackest dye; his thoughts were evil, and that continually, and his actions diabolical; the most degraded mind inhabited the most deformed body. But when an enemy falls foul upon the person, which the owner can neither make nor mend, satire becomes a kind of recommendation, for it indicates that, the features of the mind, which he *might* mend, did not afford sufficient matter for revenge. They brand him a monster from his birth, and though he came before his time, charge him as being born with all his teeth, and hair to his shoulders; however, we cannot charge him with planting either.

But Richard's character, like every other man's, had two sides; nay, in him, it comprehended two extremes, though most writers display but one, and these are best delineated by his actions.

As the prejudice of the Lancastrian writers declined, Richard's mis-shapen body, like a block of marble under the chisel of an artist, assumed a fairer form, and, brightening by degrees, he is incontestibly proved, at the end of three centuries, to have been a handsome man.

I have already remarked, he was short, and firmly built. He came into the world like other children, resembled his father in person and aspect. By his coins, pictures, and other representations he was straight. He bore a family likeness to his brother Edward, who was one of the handsomest men of the age. The Countess of Desmond, who lived to a hundred and thirty, and whose picture now graces Windsor Castle, danced with Richard in King Edward's court, and declared him "the handsomest man in the room, his brother excepted." but her feeble voice, during the sway of the Tudors, was lost in the general cry against him, for none of the old historians mention it.

While a minor, in his brother's court, he was good natured and obsequious. While governor in the north, his justice, and obliging behaviour, gained him the good will of the inhabitants. While an officer under his brother, though a boy, he displayed the most accomplished military talents; his bravery could scarcely be equalled. While a king, he was a man of business, extremely attentive to justice, and passed some singular laws for the good of the subject; such as rectifying the returns of juries, which had been shamefully abused, and attended with false verdicts; regulating bail on suspicion of felony; preserving property till conviction; and removing that hateful burthen couched, under the word *benevolence*. He was exceedingly averse to the imposition of taxes, the out-cry of every reign. His liberality was remarkable, and though his desire knew no bounds, he desired nothing but a crown. These are facts which cannot be denied by the most prejudiced person.

On the other hand, instead of giving him every excellence, let us fairly try his character upon the following accusations:

He is charged with the murder of Edward Prince of Wales, after the battle of Tewkesbury. By the best accounts ever submitted to the world there were only four persons in the room with Edward the Fourth, when Sir Richard Crofts brought in the Prince; Clarence, Dorset, Gloucester, and Hastings. The King having asked him in a majestic tone, "Why he entered his kingdom in arms?" and having received this resolute answer, "to recover my right, unjustly usurped," he struck him in the face with his gauntlet, and departed. This was considered by the courtiers, as a declaration of hostilities, and they instantly stabbed him to death. All the Lancastrian writers charge this bloody deed upon Richard. *Carte* says it was Dorset and Hastings, which is very probable, but there is no authority for either. As they were all seniors, compared to Richard, it cannot be supposed a lad of eighteen would first draw his dagger, in the presence of his superiors in age, who had always controuled him. It follows, that the unfortunate Ann Neville, daughter of the king-making Earl of Warwick, who rose to miserable greatness, by being the wife of Edward Prince of Wales; and afterwards became Queen of England, by being that of Richard the Third, has been wrongfully accused for marrying the murderer of her husband.

He is also charged with the murder of Henry the Sixth in the Tower. But it never was proved that he *was* murdered; notwithstanding the body was exhibited to public view. I will, however, for arguments sake suppose it. His life could not be worth taking by any man, particularly Richard, who had then nothing in prospect. He never had abilities, his interest was gone, his wife a prisoner, and, above all, his son was dead, without a chance of more. As the Queen was the most mischievous of the two, there would have been more policy in destroying her. Besides, the same plea of childhood holds good in this case as the last, for it happened in less then five weeks after the death of the prince.

The destruction of Clarence, in point of chronology, comes next; and though nothing criminal is proved against Richard, I am apprehensive part of the charge is just. Clarence was boisterous, and though good natured, had but little guard over his tongue. Richard was cunning, silent, eloquent at pleasure, shrewed, and designing. He early set his heart upon the crown, though many removes from it; for he considered, though there are many steps in a journey, yet for every remove the traveller makes, there is one less. Richard kept fair with all parties, and being a complete dissembler, cautiously improved the quarrel between Edward and Clarence, while he seemed the friend of both. This is in part corroborated by an expression which fell from Edward, while lamenting, when too late, the death of his brother. Intercession having been made for a criminal, he exclaimed between sorrow and anger, "how many, and urgent, applications are made, to save a wretch who ought to die by the laws of his country, but not one mouth was opened to plead for a brother in distress."

While Edward sat unsecurely on the throne, Richard was his able supporter, but when he became established by the death of Warwick, and the reduction of the Lancastrian party, Richard entertained different views, and cast his own eye towards the throne, fomented divisions among the nobility, friends to Edward, induced them to destroy each other, that should the King's demise happen, during a minority, the crown might be left open for himself; but, as before observed, it left an opening for Henry. The deaths of Gray, Rivers, Vaughan, and Hastings, were murders of the blackest dye, and are justly chargeable to Richard. His ambition was the sole cause, and Buckingham his wretched tool.

The seizure of the crown, to which he had no right, was an unjust usurpation. He was not invited to rule, but boldly obtruded himself.

Another charge is the death of Edward the Fifth, and his brother. That they were murdered, does not admit a doubt; what else could become of them? from the last intelligence, they were under Richard's care. It was no man's interest to destroy them but his. They were the only obstacles left to thwart his ambition; and though they had no power, he plainly foresaw it would arise with their years. If one or both had died a natural death, he would certainly have published it. If he was daring enough openly to remove those who were their known protectors, he would not scruple secretly to remove them. His strenuous endeavours to get the Duke of York into his power, after he had secured the King's person, point, as an index towards a diabolical design. The confession of Tyrrel and Dighton, two of their murderers, deserves attention; though rather erroneous, it throws much light on this dreadful act. We are told four persons only were concerned; Sir James Tyrrel, the temporary commandant of the Tower; John Dighton, his groom; Miles Forrest, whom Sir Thomas Moor calls a big square knave; and a priest. That ten years after, when Perkin Warbeck personated the Duke of York, it became Henry's interest to refute the imposture, by proving the murder. That Tyrrel and Dighton were apprehended, and seperately examined, in private, the other two being dead. That Henry published their confession, which declared, "that Dighton and Forrest had smothered them, in a tower, near the Water-Gate (thence called the bloody tower) with pillows, while asleep at midnight, in July 1483, and brought Tyrrel, who waited upon the stairs, to view the dead bodies when laid out, and that a priest had buried them under the stair case. That Richard dissatisfied with the place of their interment, had ordered the priest to remove them, but they could not tell where." The first part is probably true, that they were murdered and laid under the stair-case, but not by the priest. The cautious Henry believed they were destroyed, and would gladly have proved it; but had he attempted the proof, and miscarried, he would have lost than by omitting it, and Perkin would have gained what Henry lost; he therefore rested the matter upon the bare evidence of the murderers, and durst not venture to break up the ground. It follows, the latter part of the tale, which declares their interment by the priest, and their removal by Richard's order, was evidently fabricated by Henry, to prevent the hazard of a search. If one man kills another, he seldom sends for a priest to bury him. Richard was too circumspect to trust so important a secret to more than one person; nor was it of consequence to him where they were hid. The world was surprized Henry did not punish the murderers; but it would have been more surprizing if he had; for this would have destroyed that evidence he wished might exist. He knew, as they could never contradict their former assertions, they would be living witnesses in his favour; besides, a pardon, no doubt, was one of the terms of confession. This dark affair however was cleared up 192 years after the murder. March the 16th, 1675, some workmen having orders to remove a flight of stairs, leading from the King's lodgings, to the chapel in the White Tower, at the depth of nine feet, they discovered a chest of elm containing some small human bones, as Tyrrel and Dighton had described, which shews part of Henry's account to be fair. These being carefully examined, were found to be those of two boys, one about twelve, the other ten. The scull of one was whole, the other broken by the labourers, as were many of the bones, and the chest. They were then cast away with the rubbish. This being known at Court, Charles the Second ordered the rubbish to be carefully sifted, and all the bones preserved they could find, which are deposited in a marble urn, inscribed to the memory of the innocent sufferers, in Westminster Abbey. This proves Richard a villain; Henry timorous, and deceitful, the murderers confession just, and Perkin an impostor.

The death of his wife is another allegation against him. We are given to understand, "that the terms of agreement for a crown, between Henry and the people, were to unite the contending parties by marrying the princess Elizabeth; to prevent which, Richard determined to marry her himself, therefore, to clear his bed for the new bride, dispatched the old, but that the new spurned his embraces." Part of this may be relied on. That she died about that time, is certain, but it is not so certain that Richard killed her. She was far gone in a decline, had never known health since the loss of her son, a year before, nor did Richard and she live upon ill terms, he treated her with kindness; and she accompanied him in his pleasurable excursions. Besides, he was not so fond of the match as *really* to promote it; not so fond as the lady, though he might be as eager as Henry. *Carte* assures us, one of her letters to the Duke of Norfolk, is yet in the Arundel collection, wherein she intreats him to forward her nuptials with the King. Queen Elizabeth, mother to the princess, had often bespattered Richard by her sanctuary fire-side, at Westminster, and with reason. The daughter's anger must have kindled against him, in proportion to the mother's. But as the crafty Richard found means to win the mother, he would find it a much easier task to win the daughter. It remains yet to be proved, whether it is in the nature of a woman to refuse a sceptre and half a royal bed, how despicable soever the person who offers it. If she affected to despise Richard's advances, it was only like the Fox in Æsop, despising the grapes; nor did this happen in Richard's reign, but the next; when the tide of disgrace ran with such rapidity against him it was dangerous to speak in his favour. It was not so much his intentions to marry her, as a manœuvre to prevent Henry. He viewed Richmond's single attempt upon the crown as a bravado, easily crushed; but by such a marriage, a union would be effected between the Houses, and both operate against him, perhaps to destruction. Besides, he kept her a close prisoner till his death, in the castle of Sheriff-Hutton, which plainly indicated, he neither wished Henry, nor himself to marry her.

His vile attempts to prove his mother an adulteress, and his brothers bastards, if true, shews a baseness of mind, without parallel.

If Richard, as a sovereign, could justify the execution of the Duke of Buckingham, to whom he entirely owed his elevation, and that of St. Leger, his sister's husband, upon the stale principles of rebellion, yet they prove him totally void of gratitude and pity as a man.

There is but a slender barrier between the religious man and the hypocrite, and it requires a curious eye to discern it. That Richard with all his errors, had a strong tincture of religion, appears from the favour he shewed to ecclesiastics, and from his being found at devotional exercises, when solicited to take the crown. But, perhaps, we may safely pronounce this an hypocritical farce, to win the people. His charge to the judges to administer justice, and his circular letter to the Bishops for restraining vice, prove more in his favour, because the procedure was voluntary. He gave five hundred marks per annum to Queen's College in Cambridge, which farther proves a religious turn; though, perhaps, this pious act was not void of ostentation. But a more certain indication was, his fear of affronting the Virgin Mary, should he have marched on the day of her assumption.

Three natural children were the consequence of his amours, to whom he gave the name of Plantagenet, John of Gloucester, nominal governor of Calais, Catherine, who died in infancy, and a Richard, but little known in history. As all the flattering prospects of this last expired with the father, he is said, after the battle, to have hid himself in obscure life, at the early period of thirteen, and became a common day labourer, at Eastwell, in Kent, in which capacity he lived unknown, under another name, to extreme age. This is testified by some memoirs preserved in the Winchelsea family.

Former writers drew Richards character from prejudice, but as time has diminished that prejudice, their successors will, with more justice, draw it from facts. Perhaps he had a greater number of enemies than any person in the whole system of English history. It was said of Sir Robert Walpole, when he guided the helm under George the Second, "that *he* had more than any man living." But *his* were only the enemies of a day; Richard's continued for ages! They were diligent in wounding his fame, while his friends, if he had friends, were condemned to silence. – Although many crimes were laid to his charge, yet the greatest of all was *that of losing the battle of Bosworth!* This added emphasis to his guilt, gave his antagonist the ascendant, and enabled Henry to raise against him the clamour of ages. Had Richard been prosperous, he would, with all his faults, have passed through life with eclat. His errors, like those of other monarchs, would have been lost in oblivion, and himself have been handed down to posterity, as an excellent King. History would then have taken an opposite turn, and the odium have fallen upon Henry. Many of the English Princes have been as guilty as Richard, but less blamed, because more successful. The treatment of Duke Robert by his brothers, William Rufus, and Henry the First, was infinitely more diabolical, than that of Richard to Clarence. King John murdered his nephew, and his sovereign, as well as Richard, but this is little noticed by the historian, though Richard was by far the better King. Henry the Fourth stands almost excused, who really murdered Richard the Second, while our hero is condemned for the death of Henry the Sixth, though not guilty. The destruction of Warwick, by Henry the Seventh, was as vile a murder, as that of Edward the Fifth; nay, were it possible to speak in palliation of this worst of crimes, Richard was the least culpable, for he had one temptation which Henry had not: Edward the Fifth had an absolute right to the crown, but Warwick only a shadow. And the artful Queen Elizabeth, who, by her address, was idolized by the subject, and immortalized by the historian, basely destroyed a sovereign Princess, over whom she exercised power without right, Mary Queen of Scots; and, to augment the cruelty, suffered her to be insulted at the block. –

Richard's crimes originated from ambition, and took their complexion from the boldness of his character. Could he have lawfully claimed a crown, he might have made an excellent monarch; or had a crown been totally out of his reach, he might have been a valuable subject; but, placed between the two, he partook of both, and marred the subject, to make the monarch. He was a faithful servant, a brave soldier, an admirable legislator; yet one of the vilest of men. Perhaps History cannot produce an instance of such an assemblange of virtues and defects in one person. In him were united, as many excellencies as would furnish several shining characters, and as many faults as would damn a troop.

FINIS

ADDITIONAL PARTICULARS

OF THE

BATTLE OF BOSWORTH FIELD

In the additions I am about to present to the Reader, I retain the title of *Battle of Bosworth Field*; "not that this battle was fought at this place (it being fought in a large, flat, plain, and spacious ground, three miles distant from this town, between the towns of Shenton, Sutton, Dadlington, and Stoke); but for that this town was the most worthy town of note near adjacent, and was therefore called *Bosworth field*. That this battle was fought in this plain, appeareth by many remarkable places: By a little mount cast up, where the common report is, that at the first beginning of the battle Henry earl of Richmond made his parænetical oration to his army; by divers pieces of armour, weapons, and other warlike accoutrements, and by many arrow-heads here found, whereof, about 20 years since, at the inclosure of the lordship of Stoke, great store were digged up, of which some I have now [1622] in my custody, being of a long, large, and big proportion, far greater than any now in use: as also by relation of the inhabitants, who have many occurrences and passages yet fresh in memory; by reason that some persons thereabout, which saw the battle fought, were living within less than 40 years; of which persons myself have seen some, and have heard of their discourses, though related by the second hand.

"At this place king Richard III. (having brought down a great army to encounter Henry Earl of Richmond, coming from Leicester) the night before the battle pitched his tents; and, as the report hath gone, was entertained here with two unwelcome accidents; the one a prediction, the other a vision. For the first it was foretold, that if ever king Richard did come to meet his adversary in a place that was compassed with towns whose termination was in *ton**, that there he should come to great distress; or else, upon the same occasion, did happen to lodge at a place beginning and ending with the same syllable of *An* (as this of *Anbian*), that there he should lose his life, to expiate that wicked murder of his late wife Anne, daughter and

---

* "What number is adjacent, may by the Map be perceived." BURTON.

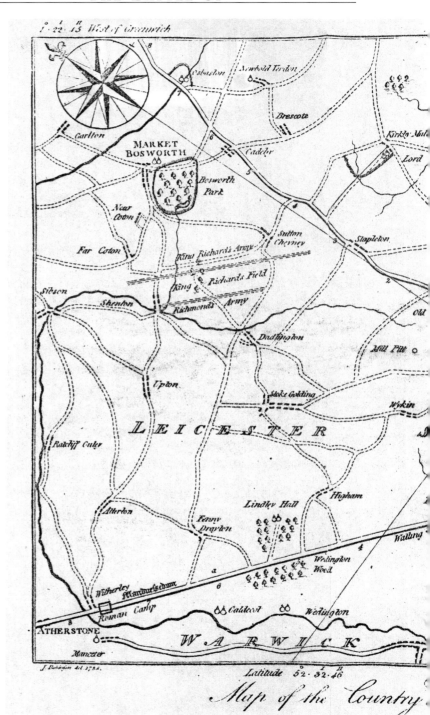

1 . 22 . 13 West of Greenwich

Carlton

MARKET BOSWORTH

Cabaston   Newbold Verdon

Brescote

Kirkby Mal.

Lord

Cadebr

Bosworth Park

Near Coton

Sutton Cheney

Stapleton

Far Coton

King Richard's Army

Sibson

Shenton

King   Richard's Field

Richmonds Army

Dadlington

Mill Pit

Old

Upton

Stoke Golding

Wykin

L E I C E S T E R

Ratcliff Culey

Higham

Lindley Hall

Atterton

Fenny Drayton

Witherley   Manduessedum

Roman Camp

ATHERSTONE

Manceter

Welington Wood

Walling

Caldcot   Wedington

W A R W I C K

J. Robinson del. 1785.

Latitude 52 . 32 . 46

Map of the Country

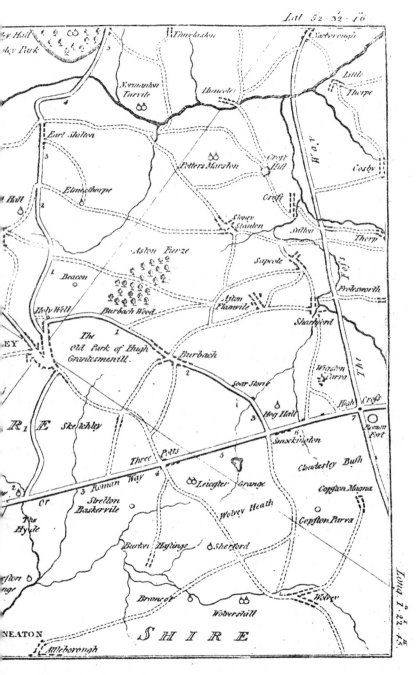

coheir of Richard Nevile earl of Salisbury and Warwick. The vision is reported to be in this manner: King Richard lying in his tent, there appeared unto him divers fearful ghosts, running about him, not suffering him to take any rest, still crying revenge; which vision he related to his friends in the morning. But Polydore Vergil, in his English History, in the life of king Richard III. will not have this to be any vision or dream at all, but only a guilty conscience. His word are these: 'Verùm id credo non fuit somnium, sed conscientia scelerum; conscientia, inquam, eò gravior, quò culpa major, quæ, si aliàs nunquam, at extremo vitæ die, solet nobis commissa nostra representare, ac illorum simul impendentes pœnas monstrare, ut meritò ad id temporis punctum malè actæ vitæ pœnitentes hinc tristes migrare cogamur.' And assuredly there is no defence or shield like to a good conscience, nor a crueller torment than a evil conscience; as well he hath observed it, upon the many vile plots and cruel murders by the said king Richard committed; as the violent death of king Henry VI. and of Edward prince of Wales his son; king Edward V. and his brother Richard duke of York, his brother's sons; queen Anne his wife, Henry duke of Buckingham, William lord Hastings, Anthony earl Rivers, sir Richard Grey, and many others. Another accident here happened to John Howard duke of Norfolk, a chief friend of king Richard; who having a caveat given him by a rhyming distich (as the vulgar Chroniclers say) fixed upon his pavilion; but (as the more received report goeth) by a letter thrown into his tent, discovering the falling off of the puissant lord Stanley, and the revolt of many others of the nobles; which he, whether upon a strong assurance of the king's power, or the touch of his own allegiance, or, perhaps, deferment of the reading thereof to some fitter time, neglected the perusal, and consequence thereof; and so, with the king, was there slain; like to Julius Cæsar, who, as he was going to the Senate-house, had a libel delivered to him by Artemidorus, a philosopher of Cnidos (as it is in Plutarch), one of the conspirators, and a familiar of Brutus the arch-traitor, discovering all the plot and circumstances thereof: which he, then neglecting to take view thereof, put into his bosom, reserving it to some fit opportunity, and was in the said house then slain."

Thus far I have given the exact words of Mr. Burton, the original Historian of Leicestershire, a great part of it transcribed in 1810 from his till then unpublished MS. But I shall doubtless stand excused for entering more particularly into the history of an event so important in the English Annals.

The plain called *Bosworth Field* is spacious; and, being very nearly surrounded with hills and woods, has a beautifully noble appearance. The woods of Sutton Chainell and of Anbien, in particular, have a striking effect; but *no pillar* is erected to commemorate the event*. The place famed for one of the most important events in the English Annals is only ascertained by oral tradition.

The short but eventful reign of king Richard III. commenced June 23, 1483; and, after having been regularly crowned at Westminster on the 6th of July, Richard thought it prudent to make a progress into the North, through Windsor, Oxford, and Conventry, to Leicester, whence several of his warrants in that year, from the 17th to the 19th of August, are dated.

One of this is here copied:

"Richard, by the grace of God, &c. To all our officers, legemen, and subgetts, to whom o' letters shall be shewed, greting. Forsemech as we have co'manded o' trusty squier and servant Nicholas Spicer, one of thousshers of our chambre, for to doo ii thousand Walshe billes in all hast possible to be p'oveyd' and made for us (and by these presents have geven unto him power and autorite for to take, in our name, in any place where him shall seme most expedient, as many smythes as shall be by him be thought necessarye for thaccomplishing enne extent in yt behalve): we therefore will and charge you all and eny of you that unto our said servant, o' such as by him shalle be assigned thereunto, ye be obeieng, helping, and assisting, in all wise as it apperteynethe, w^{th}owt failling, as ye well answere unto us at yo' perill. Yeven at Leicestre, the xvii^{th} day of August, ye first yere of our reigne†."

From Leicester the new Monarch proceeded, through Nottingham, to York; whence, preparatory to a second coronation, he sent an order on the 31st of August to Piers Courteys, the keeper of his wardrobe, for an immense cargo of "extraordinary garniture;" and the ceremony was solemnly performed, in the beginning of September, in the Chapter-house, by the archbishop; of which a full account is preserved by Mr. Drake, in his "History of York."

* On this subject, see the Preface to the present Volume.

† Preserved among the Harleian MSS. in the British Museum, No. 433. p. 110. b.

The attentions which the King received in that antient city were requited by some especial grants and immunities; but in the short period of two months, the good citizens of York had notice from the king, Oct. 11, 1483, "that the duke of Buckingham had traiterously turned upon him, contrary to the duty of his legiaunce*."

April 11, 1484, another letter was addressed by the king to the magistrates of York, giving an account of "the number of lyes and contumelious speeches which were then spread abroad against him†."

That the pretensions of the earl of Richmond soon afterward began to give alarm, is evident from the following mandate to the mayor of Windsor:

"R. Rex. By the King.
Trusty and well beloved, we greet you well. And for as much as wee be credibly informed, that our rebells and traytours, now confedered wth our antient enemies of France, by many and sundry wayes conspire and study the meanes to ye subvercon' of this our realme, and of unity amongst our subjects; as in tending writings, by seditious persons, wth counterfeyt and contrive false invenc'ons, tydings, and rumours, to th' intent to provoke and stirre discord and division betwixt us and our Ll^ds, which be as faithfully disposed as any subjects can suffice: Wee therfore will and co'mande you streigthly, that, in eschewing of the incovenients abovesaid, you put you in uttermost devoire, if any such rumours or writings come amongst you, to search and enquire of the first shewers and utterers thereof: And y^em that ye shall soe find ye doe co'mitt unto sure warde; and after proceed to theyr sharp punishm^t, in example and feare of all other, not failing hereof in any wise as ye entend to please us, and will answere unto us at your perills. Yeoven under our signett, at our palace of Westm^r, ye 6 day of December [1484]§."

From the high-spirited and gallant earl of Richmond, we soon after find the following manifesto:

*Drake's History of York, p. 118.

† Drake's History of York, p. 119.

§ Harl. MSS. 787, fol. 2. b.

"Henry e. of Richm^d, before he was k. to his freinds here in Engl^d, from beyond the seas, &c.

R^t trusty, wor'p'll, and hon'ble good freinds and our allyes, I greet you well. Being given to understand your good devoir and intent to advance me to ye furtherance of my rightfull claime, due and lineall inheritance of ye crowne; and for ye just depriving of that homicide and unnatural tyrant wch now unjustly bears dominion over you: I give you to understand, y^t noe Christian heart can be more full of ioye and gladnes, then ye heart of me yor poore exiled ffriend, who will, upon ye instance of your sure advertise what powers ye will make ready, and what captains and leaders you gett to conduct, be prepared to pass over ye sea wth such forces as my ffreindes here are preparing for me. And if I have such good speed and success as I wish according to your desire, I shall ever be most forward to remember, and wholly to requite, this your great and most lovinge kindness in my just quarrell. Yeoven under our signett.

HR

I pray you give credence to ye messenger of y^t he shall impart to you*."

In a letter addressed to the people of England, dated Westminster, June 23, 1485, Richard artfully persuades them "to resist Henry Tudor, and his attainted traitors, whom he pronounces murderers, adulterers, extortioners, rebels to God, honour, and nature; who obey his antient enemy the French king; and, under Henry their bastard leader, begotten in double adultery, intend to enter his kingdom, and, by conquest, despoil his subjects of life, liberty, and goods; to destroy all the honourable blood in the realm, and seize their possessions: therefore advises every man to lift up his hand against them†."

An order occurs among the records at York, July 8, for the citizens to be "defensibly arrayed;" and on the 16th of August it was directed, that "John Spon, sergeant to the mase, should ride to Nottingham, to the King's Grace, to understand his pleasure in

---

* Harl. MSS. 787, fol. 2. b.

† See this Letter at large in Mr. Hutton's "History of Bosworth Field," p. 65.

sending up any of his subjects within the city of York, for the subduing of his enemies lately arrived in the parts of Wales, or otherwise to be disposed at his most high pleasure;" and on the 19th, in consequence of a message from the king, from Beskwood, "400 men, defensibly arrayed, John Hastings gentleman of the mace being captain, were ordered, in all haste possible, to depart towards the King's Grace, for the subduing of his enemies*."

On Sunday, July 31, 1485, Richmond set sail from Harfleur; landed at Milford Haven on the 6th of August; and marched, through Wales, by Dell, Haverfordwest, Cardigan, New Town, and Welsh Pool, to Shrewsbury, and thence, through Newport and Stafford, to Lichfield, where he encamped for a day or two, and then proceeded to Tamworth, where his army arrived late in the evening of August 18; but he himself, following in the rear with about twenty horsemen, missed his road, and passed the night solitarily at a little village three miles distant. Early on the 19th, after shewing himself at Tamworth to his army, he had an interview with his father-in-law lord Stanley at Atherstone, when measures were concerted for the future operations; and in the evening he was joined by sir John Savage, sir Bryan Sanford, sir Simon Digby, and many other experienced warriors. On the 20th, Richmond encamped at Atherstone; and on the 21st both armies were in sight of each other for the whole day.

Richard, despising the supposed weakness of his adversary, yet desiring effectually to crush him, led his army, on the 16th, in great regal state, from Nottingham castle to Leicester; which town he entered in open pomp, the crown-royal on his head; and on the 17th, quitted it, in the same manner, expecting to meet his rival at Hinckley. That night he passed at Elmsthorpe, where his officers slept in the Church. On the 18th he marched to Stapleton, where he pitched his camp on ground called *The Bradshaws*, where he continued till Sunday the 21st, when both armies came in sight of each other. In the evening Richard removed to *Anbein hill*, where "he pitched his field, refreshed his soldiers, and took his rest†." The next morning early, bringing all his men out of the camp into the

---

* Drake's History of York, p. 120.

† "Richard is thought to have despised his enemy too much, and been too dilatory in his motions. (See the Notes on the Paston Letters.) As the contest was almost

plain, he ordered both horsemen and footmen to be drawn up in a length of line, that their numbers might appear as large as possible. The archers were placed in the front, under the command of the duke of Norfolk and his son the earl of Surrey. This long vanguard was followed by Richard himself with a chosen band, supported on each side with wings of horsemen. The whole number exceeded 16,000.

The army of Richmond, which amounted not to 5000, was proportionally arranged by their gallant leader. The archers, in a narrow front, were led by the earl of Oxford; the right wing was entrusted to sir Gilbert Talbot, the left to sir John Savage. Richmond himself reserved a good company of horse, and a small number of foot.

On each side the leader addressed his troops with a splendid oration; "which was scarcely finished," says an old Historian, "but the one army espied the other. Lord! how hastily the soldiers buckled their helms, how quickly the archers bent their bows, and brushed their feathers – how readily the billmen shook their bills and proved their staves*, ready to approach and join when the terrible trumpet should sound the bloody blast to victory or death!

personal, the Royal Commanders should in prudence have kept out of danger; but, for the same reason, were obliged to encounter the greatest, as they could not decently desire their followers to do for them what they themselves would not do for themselves, who alone were to be benefited. It is the case of Cyrus and Artaxerxes: only that the invader succeeded. In such cases the judgment would be, to appoint a band of determined men to lay by till they could see where the opposite Commanders were; with orders to fight neither with great nor small, but him only, as all depends upon his death. It seems that Richard attempted somewhat of this kind; but he should not have been of the party himself, unless we suppose that Richard had alienated the minds of some of his chief followers, as certainly was the case of Stanley. His own known character as a soldier, his superiority in numbers, and, as one should suppose, better appointed, must have secured him the victory; but, as Voltaire remarks, every invader of England succeeds: luckily, the last proved an exception to the rule." G. ASHBY. – May all future attempts at invasion prove equally abortive!

* So Shakspeare, "See that my staves be sound." Churchyard, mentioning an action in which he was, says, "None of the English returned without having broken two or three staves." In tilting I understand this, not in battle. G. ASHBY.

Between both armies there was a great morass, which the earl of Richmond left on his right hand for this intent, that it should be on that side a defence for his part; and in so doing he had the sun at his back, and in the faces of his enemies."

The first conflict of the archers being over, the armies met fiercely with swords and bills; and at this period Richmond was joined by lord Stanley, which determined the fortune of the day. In this battle (which lasted little more than two hours) above one thousand persons were slain on the side of Richard. Of Richmond's army scarcely 100 were slain; among whom the principal person was sir William Brandon, his standard-bearer.

The victor was crowned in the field by sir William Stanley, with a crown of ornament which Richard wore in the battle, and which was found by sir Reginald Bray* among the spoils. A tradition remains that it was secreted in a bush on his hill†.

After the battle, Henry VII. went to Coventry with his army, and lodged at the mayor's house (by name Robert Onley), whom he knighted; at which time the city presented him with 100 *l*. and a cup§.

"On the 23d of August, it was shewed by divers persons, especially by John Spon, sent unto the field of Redmore to bring tidings from the same to the city, that king Richard, late *lawfully* reigning over us, was, through great treason of the duke of Norfolk, and many others that turned against him, with many other lords and nobility of the North parts, *piteously slain and murdered*, to the great hevines of this city; it was therefore determined, at the *wofull season*, to apply to the earl of Northumberland for advice‡."

On the 24th, it appeared that the earl of Northumberland was with king Henry at Leicester; in whose name a proclamation was

---

* Gent. Mag. 1789, vol. LIX. p. 424.

† "Richard wore his crown openly with design. It could not therefore be secreted till after his fall; and, when once separated from his head, might be run away with, and hid any where close to, or more likely at a distance from, where the king fell." G. ASHBY.

§ Dugdale, Warwickshire, vol. I. p. 143.

‡ Drake's History of York, p. 121.

made, on the 25th, for preservation of the peace; which thus concludes: "Moreover, the King assertayneth you, that Richard late duke of Gloucester, late called king Richard, was slain at a place called *Sandeford*, within the shire of Leicester, and brought dead off the field unto the town of Leicester, and there was laid openly, that every man might see and look upon him; and also there was slain, upon the same field, John late duke of Norfolk, John late earl of Lincoln, Thomas late earl of Surrey, Francis Viscount Lovell, sir Walter Devereux lord Ferreres, Richard Ratcliff knight, Robert Brakenbury knight, with many other knights, squiers, and gentlemen; *of whose soules God have mercy**."

The subsequent important events are fully detailed by most of our English Historians; but the following narrative is now first printed from a MS. preserved in the British Museum†; the title of which states it to have been "borowyd of Henry Savyll:"

"When Henri erle of Richmond cam in at Mylford Haven, he sayd thes words: 'A! Yngland, I am enteryd here to clayme myne heritage. Jhesu, that dyed on Good Friday, and Mary his mothar, send me the love of the Lord. Stanley he hathe maried my mothar; it is longe sithe she saw me; I trust to Jesus we shall mete, and our brother syr William Stanley.'

"Let us leve Henry, and speke of Richard in his dignitie, and the mysfortune that hym befell: a wicked cownsell drew hym.

"The lord Stanley, sterne and stowte, he may be callyd flowre in his cuntrye, and that was well sene at Barwicke, when all the lords of England let it be that castle wightly cowlde he wine; than of kynge Richard toke he leve, and set good rule amonge the comon'tie; but wicked cownsell drew Richard ...... Thes was the words they sayd to hym: 'We thinke yow worke unwitily in England, if ye wold contynew kynge; for bothe lord Stanley, lord Strange, and the Chamberlayne, thes iii may bringe agaynst yow on a day, that no lords may in England far nor nere, and the sonns of the mother that are banished may caws yow short tyme to were the crowne.' Then k. Richard made owt mesengars far into the West contrie to the lord Stanley, to repayr to hym with spede. Then the lord Stanley bowned

---

* Drake's History of York, p. 122.

† Harl. MSS. 542. fol. 34.

hym toward kyng Rychard; but he fell sycke at Manchestar by the waye, as was the wyll of God. To the lord Strange then callyd he, and sayd thes words to hym: 'In goodly haste bowne must ye to wyt the will of Richard owr kyng.' The ...... Lord Strange bownyd him to ryde to kynge Richard. When he cam before hym, and knelyd downe, kynge Richard sayd, 'Welcome lord Stange, and kynsman neare; wher is any lord in England of aunsitry shuld be so trew to his kynge?' Ther was no more of this to say, but to ward commandyd was he; and messengars wer made into the West contry, to the lord Stanley. Thes wer the words they sayd to hym: 'Yow must rayse up undar yowr bannar to mayntayne Rychard owr kynge, for yondar comythe Richmond ovar the flode with many an alyannt owt of far contry, to chalandge the crowne of England; yow most reyse that undar yowr bannar be with the noble powere that yow may brynge, or els the lord Strange yow moste never se, that is in danger of our kynge.' In a studye still then that lord did stond, and say, 'Jesu, how may this be? I take wittes of Hym that shope both se and sande, I never delt with traytorie; Richard is the man that hathe no mercye; he wold me and myne bondage bringe; therefor agaynst hym will I be.' Another messengar came to William Stanley, that noble knyght, and sayd, 'K. Richard warethe y^e to bringe thy royal tent; his hope is holy therin.' Then answeryd the noble knyght, 'I marvayle of our kyng: he hathe my nevyew, my brothar's heire; a trewar knyght is not in Christinte: he shall repent, by eny thyng that I can se well. K. Richard this, for all the power that he can bringe, he shall eyther fight or fle, or lose his lyfe. I make a vow, I shall give him suche a brekefast on a day as never knyght gave kynge. Therefor, byde hym aray hym and his power; for he shall ethar fyght or fle, or lose his lyfe.' Then the messengar rydes to the king, and saythe, 'In the contry wher I have be, men so grevyd I nevar se for the lord Strange sake, that in bale doth lye; they say they will cawse you to fight or flye, or els to lose your lyfe.' Kynge Richard smyled, and swore, by ......when they be sembled all, 'I wold the great Turke wer agaynst me, with Prester John, and the Sowdan of Surre, with all theyr powers: for all theyr manhod I wold be kynge.' He swore, by Jesu and his mothar, 'that, from the town of Lancastre to Shrowsberye, knyght ne sqwire, he wold live none alyve, and he wold deal theyr lands to his knyghtes, from the Holy Heade to Seynt David's land; wheras ar castells and towers hye, I shall make parkes and playne fields: frithe and forest fre, they shall all repent that evar he rose agaynst his kynge.' Then he sent out messengars, bothe far and nyghe, to deuke, earle, baron, knyght, and othar in ther degre. Part of theyr names shall yow here that came to kynge Richard; the duke of Northfolke, the erle of Surrey his heyre, the erle of Kent, the erle of Shrowsbery, the erle of Northumbarland, the erle of Westmerland, Robert Rydyssh, sir Robert Owtrege, sir John Huntyngton, sir John Wilinn, sir John Smalby, sir Bryan of Stapleton, sir William his cosen, the lord Fryn so gray, the lord Lovell chamberlayn of England, the lord Hughe his cosyn, the lord Scrope of Yposall, the lord Scrope of Bolton; the lord Dakers raysed the North contrye; the lord Owgle; the lord Bower; the lorde Graystoke, he browght a myghty many; sir John Blekynson, sir Raffe Harebotley, sir William Warde, syr Archebald with the good Rydley; syr Nycholas Nabogay was not awaye; sir Olyver of Chaston, sir Henry de hynd Horsay, sir John de Gray, sir Thomas de Mingumbre, sir Roger Standfort, Sir Robert Bracanberye, sir Harry Landringam, sir Richard Chorwlton, sir Raffe Rolle, Sir Thomas Marcomfild, sir Rogar Sandyll, sir Christofer Ward, sir William Beckfort, sir John Cowburne, sir Robert Plwmton, sir William Gaskoyne, sir Marmaduke Constable, sir William Conyers, sir Martin of the Fee, sir Robart Gilbard, sir Richard Heaton, sir John Lothes, sir Willyam Ratclyf, sir Thomas his brothar, sir Willyam theyr brothar, sir Christofer de Mallyre, sir John Norton, sir Thomas de Mallyveray, sir Raffe Dakers of the Northe, sir Christofer the Morys, sir William Musgrave, sir Alexander Haymor, sir George Mortynfield, sir Thomas Browghton, sir Christofer Awayne, sir Richard Tempest out of the Dale, sir William his cosyn, sir Raffe of Ashton, sir Roger Long in Arpenye, sir John Pudsay, sir Robart of Mydleton, sir Thomas Stryckland, sir John Nevill of Bloodfallhye, sir John Adlyngton, sir Roger Hearon, sir James Harryngton, sir Robart his brothar, sir Thomas Pilkylton. All thes sware kynge Richard shuld were the crowne.

"Now shall I tell how Henry of Richmond cam to the crowne. The lorde Stanley from Lathom castle upon a day bownyd he, with knyghts and esquiers in his company, with theyr bannars, fearce to fyght, to mantayn Henry to be theyr kynge. To the New Castell undar Lyne this lorde toke the way, with his noble men in companye; he told them wagys the noble powers that he dyd brynge. Sir William Stanley, that noble knyght, from the Castell of the Holt to the Northwycke he rode, and told his men wagis all the Northe Wayles the most part, and the flower of Chestar, which he did brynge earlye on a Sonday at morne. Sir William of Stanley removyd from the

Northewicke to the towne of Stone. By then was Henry come to Stafford; and a prevy message sent he to hym with a certayn parson. That noble knyght rod to Stafford toward the kynge. When that he saw the prince in syght, he knelyd downe, and hent hym by the hand; and said, 'I am more glade of the then all the gold in Crystentye; I trust to the lord my father and ye that in England I shal be kynge.' Then the othar sayd, 'Welcome, Soveraygne Kynge Henry; chalendge thye heritage, and this land; loke thow fyght, and nevar flye: remembar anothar day who dothe for thee, yf thow be kynge.' Leve of the prince tane, he came agayn, by the lyght of the day, unto the lytle towne of Stone, early on a Saturday. To Lychfeld removyd old and yonge. At Worsley bredge ther beforne, they had a syght of Henry that shuld be kynge. Unto Lychefild they ryde; a harrot of armes came to number the company that was with the knyght; it was a goodly syght; gonnes in Lychefyld craked; glad was all the chevalry that was on Henry's party. Througheout Lychefyld rydes that knyght; and on the othar syd taryed he, tyll a nessage cam to hym, and sayd, 'Lord Stanley is his inemyes nye; they be but a lytle way atwyne; he will fight within thes thre howres with Richard of England, callyd kyng.' 'That wold I not (quod the knyght) for all the world in Cristentie;' and toward Tanworth he toke the way. He came to Adorstone ere nyght, wher the lord Stanley lay in a dale, with trompets, and a goodly company: all that nyght they ther abode. Upon Sunday they hard masse; and to a fayr field toke the way; the vaward lord Stanley had, his brothar sir William in the rereward, his sonne Edward in a wynge. Then came prince Henry. It was a goodly syght to see the metyng of them, the lorde and the kynge. Upon a bay courser was the kinge, a lytle before the nyght. On the morrow, when the larke gan synge, kynge Henry askyd the waward of the lord Stanley, which he grawntyd, and lent to him iiii knyghts to go with hym to the vaward, Gilbert Talbut, John Savage, sir Hughe Percivall, and sir George Stanley; thes arayed them to the vaward with the kynge; the lord Stanley the second batail had; sir William Stanley he was the hyndermoste at the first settyng. Then they removyd to a hyghe mountayne; and, lokyng into a dale of ...... myles coompasse, they saw no syght for armyd men and traped steds in iiii battayls. The duke of Norfolke advansyd his bannar; so dyd yonge erle of Shrisberye, and erle of Oxford*. The kyng Richard had vii skore sargents that wer cheyned and lockyd in a row, and as many bumbards, and thousands

---

* "The erle of Oxford was on kyng Henry's syde."

of morys pyks, haggebushes, &c. Kyng Richard lookyd into a mountayne hye, and saw the bannar of the lord Stanley, and sayd, 'Fetche the lord Strange to me, or els he shall dye this day.' They brought the lord unto his syght, and he said, 'For thy deathe make the redy.' Then answaryd that noble knyght, and sayde, 'I cry God and the world mercy. Ihesus, I take to witnes, that I was nevar traytor to my kynge.' Upon a gentelman then called he, Lathome was his name; 'and evar ye come into my contrie, grete well my gentellmen and yomen; they had a mastar, now have they none.' Then he drew a rynge of his fingar, and sayd, 'Give this to my ladye; if the field be lost on our partye, take my sonne that is myne heire, and fly into a far contrye.' Then came a knyght to kynge Richard, and sayd, 'It is highe tyme to loke about; loke how yowr vaward begynethe to fyght. When ye have the fathar and sonne the yeman, loke yow what deathe they shall dye: ye may head all at yowr own will.' With that fortunate worde they counteryd together full egarly. Whan the vaward began to fight, kynge Henry dyd full manfully; so dyd the erle of Oxford, so dyd sir John Savage; sir Gilbert Talbot dyd the lyke; sir Hughe Percivall also, with many othar. Kynge Richard, in a marris, dyd stand nombred to xx thousand and thre undar his bannar. Sir William Stanley remembringe the brekfast that he promysed hym, downe at a banke he hyed, and set fiersly on the kynge: they counteryd together sadly. The archers let theyr arrows flye; they shot of goonns; many a bannar began to show that was on Richard's partye; with grownd wepons they joyned: there dyed many a dowghty knyght. Then to kyng Richard ther cam a knyght, and sayd, 'I hold it tyme for ye to flye; yondar Stanley his dynts be so sore, agaynst them may no man stand. Her is thy hors for to ryde: an othar day ye may worshipe wyne.' He said, 'Bryng me my battayl axe in my hand, and set the crowne of gold on my hed so hye; for by hym that shope bothe se and sand, kynge of England this day will I dye; one foote away I will not fle, whill brethe wyll byde my brest within.' As he sayd, so dyd he; he lost his lyffe. On his standard then fast they dyd lyght. They hewyd the crowne of gold from his hed with dowtfull dents: his deathe was dyght. The duke of Norfolke dyd flye; the lord Surrey, with many othar mo. And boldly on bere they dyd hym brynge. And many a noble knyght then lost theyr lyffe with Richard theyr kynge. There was slayn syr Richard Ratcliff, one of kynge Richard's counsell; syr William Conyers, ser Robart of Brackanbery, syr Richard of Charrington. Amongst all othar, I remember tow, sir William Brand was the one of tho; kynge Henry's standard he hevyd on hye, and vamisyd it, tyll with deathe's dent he was stryken downe. Syr Richard

Percivall, Thurleball the othar hight, kynge Richard's standard he kept on hyghe, tyll bothe his leggs wer cut hym fro; yet to the grownd he wold not let it goo, whill brethe was in his brest. Then they removyd to a mountayne hyghe, and with a voice they cryed *Kynge Henry*. The crowne of gold was delyveryd to the lord Stanley; and unto kynge Henry then went he, and delyveryd it, as to the most worthe to were the crowne and be theyre kynge. They brought kynge Richard thethar that nyght, as nakyd as evar he was borne, and in the New Warke was he layd, that many a man might se," &c.

Richard, it is universally acknowledged, performed prodigies of valour. Desperate, perhaps, at the last, he rushed furious into the thickest of the fight, slew numbers, and among them the standard-bearer of Richmond, with his own hand; and fell at last, ingloriously (if tradition may be credited), by a treacherous blow from one of his own followers. His body was thrown across a horse, and carried for interment to the Grey Friars at Leicester.

"After revenge and rage had satiated their barbarous cruelties upon his dead body, they gave his royal earth a bed of earth, honourably, appointed by the order of King Henry the Seventh, in the chief Church of Leicester, called St. Mary's, belonging to the order and society of the Grey Friers; the King in short time after causing a fair tomb of mingled-coloured marble, adorned with his statue, to be erected thereupon; to which some grateful pen had also destined an epitaph, the copy whereof (never fixed to his stone) I have seen in a recorded manuscript book chained to a table in a chamber in the Guildhall of London, which (the faults and corruptions amended) is thus represented, together with the title thereunto prefixed, as I found it:

'Epitaphium Regis Richardi Tertii, sepulti ad Leicestriam, jussu et sumptibus S[ti] Regis henrici Septimi.

> Hic ego, quem vario tellus sub marmore claudit,
> Tertius a justâ[a] voce Richardus eram.
> Tutor eram patriæ[b], patrius pro jure nepotis;
> Diruptâ, tenui regna Britanna, fide.
> Sexaginta dies binis duntaxat ademptis
> Æstatesque tuli tunc[c] mea sceptra duas.
> Fortiter in bello certans[d] desertus ab Anglis,
> Rex Henrice, tibi, septime, succubui.
> At sumptu, pius ipse, tuo, sic ossa dicaras[e],

Regem olimque facis regis honore coli.

Quatuor exceptis jam tantum, quinque bis annis,

Acta trecenta quidem, lustra salutis erant.

Anteque Septembris undenâ luce kalendas,

Reddideram rubræ jura petita[f] Rosæ.

At mea, quisquis eris, propter commissa precare,

Sit minor ut precibus pœna levata[g] tuis.'

*** Various readings in this epitaph, in a copy given by Sandford, p. 435, from the Heralds' College MSS. vol. I. p. 3:

[a] Multa.

[b] Nam patriæ tutor.

[c] Non.

[d] Merito.

[e] Decoras.

[f] Dedita jura.

[g] Fienda.

Englished:

'I who am laid beneath this marble stone,

Richard the Third, possess'd the British Throne.

My Country's Guardian in my Nephew's claim,

By trust betray'd I to the Kingdom came.

Two years and sixty days, save two, I reign'd;

And bravely strove in fight; but, unsustain'd,

My English left me in the luckless field,

Where I to Henry's arms was forc'd to yield.

Yet at his cost my corse this Tomb obtains,

Who piously interr'd me, and ordains

That Regal honours wait a King's remains.

Th'year thirteen hundred 'twas and eighty-four,

The twenty-first of August, when its power

And all its rights I did to the Red Rose restore.

Reader, whoe'er thou art, thy prayers bestow,

T'atone my crimes, and ease my pains below*.'

* Buck's Richard III. in the "Complete History of England," vol. I. p. 577.

"The wicked and tyrannical prince king Richard III. being slain at Bosworth, his body was begged by the nuns [friers] at Leicester (alitèr Grey friers), and buried in their chapel there; at the dissolution whereof, the place of his burial happened to fall into the bounds of a citizen's garden; which being (after) purchased by Mr. Robert Heyrick (some time mayor of Leicester), was by him covered with a handsome stone pillar, three feet high, with this inscription: 'Here lies the body of Richard III. some time king of England.' This he shewed me (Christopher Wren, B.D.) walking in the garden, 1612*."

The Rev. Samuel Carte, vicar of St. Martin's in Leicester, says, in 1720, "I know no other evidence that the stone coffin formerly used for a horse-trough was king Richard's, but the constancy of the tradition. There is a little part of it still preserved at the White Horse Inn, in which one may observe some appearance of the hollow, fitted for retaining the head and the shoulders."

Mr. Throsby adds, "When I was a boy, the end that then remained stood as a part of a heap of rubbish, in the inn-yard, of brick-ends, stones, &c."

"King Richard the Third, before the Battle of Bosworth, rode through the South gate [of Leicester]; a poor old blind man (by profession a wheelwright) sat begging, and, hearing his approach, said, that if the Moon changed twice that day, having by her ordinary course changed in the morning, king Richard should lose his crown, and be slain: And a nobleman that carried the Moon for his colours revolted; thereby he lost his life and kingdom†."

Michael Drayton, who lived in the neighbourhood of the Battle, thus apostrophises:

---

* Wren's Parentalia, p. 114.

† "Tenne strange Prophecies," &c. 1644.

"Then, Bosworth, here the Muse now lastly bids for thee
Thy Battle to describe, the last of that long War,
Entitled by the name of York and Lancaster,
'Twixt Henry Tudor earl of Richmond, only left
Of the Lancastrian line, who by the Yorkists rest
Of liberty at home, a banish'd man abroad,
In Britanny had liv'd; but late at Milford road
Being prosperously arriv'd, though scarce two thousand strong,
Made out his way through Wales, where, as he came along,
First Griffith great in blood, then Morgan next doth meet
Him, with their several powers, as offering at his feet
To lay their lands and lives; Sir Rice ap Thomas then,
With his brave band of Welsh most choice and expert men,
Comes lastly to his aid. At Shrewsbury arriv'd,
(His hopes, so faint before, so happily reviv'd)
He on for England makes, and near to Newport town
The next ensuing night setting his army down,
Sir Gilbert Talbot still for Lancaster that stood
(To Henry near allied in friendship as in blood)
From th' earl of Shrewsbury his nephew (under age)
Came with two thousand men in warlike equipage,
Which much his power increased; when easily setting on
From Lichfield as the way leads forth to Atherston,
Brave Bourcher and his friend stout Hungerford, whose hopes
On Henry long had lain, stealing from Richard's troops,
(Wherewith they had been mix'd) to Henry do appear,
Which with a high resolve most strangely seemed to cheer
His oft appalled heart. But yet the man which most
Gave sayle to Henry's self, and fresh life to his host,
The stout lord Stanley was, who for he had affide
The mother of the earl, to him so near allied,
The King, who fear'd his truth, (which he to have, compell'd)
The young lord Strange his son in hostage strongly held,
Which forc'd him to fall off, till he fit place could find
His son-in-law to meet; yet with him he combin'd
Sir William Stanley, known to be a valiant knight,
T'assure him of his aid. Thus growing tow'rds his height,
A most selected band of Cheshire bow-men came,
By sir John Savage led, besides two mwn of name,
Sir Brian Sanford, and sir Simon Digby, who,
Leaving the Tyrant King, themselves expressly shew
Fast friends to Henry's part, which still power increas'd
Both armies, well prepar'd, tow'rds Bosworth strongly prest,
And a spacious moor, lying Southward from the town,
Indifferent to them both, they set their armies down
Their soldiers to refresh, preparing for the fight:
Where to the guilty King, that black fore-running night,
Appear the dreadful ghosts of Henry and his Son,
Of his own brother George, and his two nephews done

Most cruelly to death; and of his wife, and friend
Lord Hastings, with pale hands prepar'd as they would rend
Him piece-meal; at which of the roareth in his sleep.
No sooner 'gan the dawn out of the East to peep,
But drums and trumpets chide the soldiers to their arms,
And all the neighb'ring fields are cover'd with the swarms
Of those that came to fight, as those that came to see
(Contending for a Crown) whose that great day should be.
First, Richmond rang'd his fights, on Oxford and bestows
The leading, with a band of strong and sinewy bows
Out of the army pick'd; the front of all the field,
Sir Gilbert Talbot next, he wisely took to wield
The right wing with his strengths, most Northern men that were;
And sir John Savage, with the power of Lancashire
And Cheshire (chief of men), was for the left wing plac'd;
The middle battle he in his fair person grac'd;
With him the noble earl of Pembroke, who commands
Their countrymen the Welsh, (of whom it mainly stands,
For their great numbers found to be of greatest force
Which, but his guard of gleaves, consisted all of horse.
Into two several fights the King contriv'd his strength,
And his first battle cast into a wondrous length,
In fashion of a wedge, in point of which he set
His archery, thereof and to the guidance let
Of John the noble duke of Norfolk, and his son
Brave Surry: he himself the second bringing on,
Which was a perfect square; and on the other side
His horsemen had for wings, which, by extending wide,
The adverse seem'd to threat with an unequal power.
The utmost point arriv'd of this expected hour,
He to lord Stanley sends, to bring away his aid,
And threats him by an oath, if longer he delay'd,
His eldest son young Strange immediately should die;
To whom stout Stanley thus doth carelessly reply:
'Tell thou the King, I'll come when I fit time shall see;
I love the boy, but yet I have more sons than he.'
The angry armies meet, when the thin air was rent
With such re-echoing shouts from either's soldiers sent,
That flying o'er the field the birds down trembling dropt
As some old building, long that hath been underpropt,
When as the timber fails, by the unwieldy fall
E'en into powder beats the roof and rotten wall,
And with confused clouds of smould'ring dust doth choke
The streets and places near; so through the misty smoke,
By shot and ordenance made, a thund'ring noise was heard.
When Stanley, that this while his succours had deferr'd
Both to the cruel King, and to the Earl his son,
When once he doth perceive the battle was begun,
Brings on his valiant troops, three thousand fully strong,

Which, like a cloud far off, that tempest threaten'd long,
Falls on the Tyrant's host, which him with terror struck:
As also when he sees he doth but vainly look
For succours from the great Northumberland this while,
That, from the battle scarce three quarters of a mile,
Stood with his power of horse, nor once was seen to stir;
When Richard (that the events no longer would defer,
The main two battles mix'd, and that with wearied breath
Some labour'd to their life, some labour'd to their death,
Therefore the better fought) e'en with a spirit elate,
As one that inly scorn'd the very worst that Fate
Could possibly impose, his lance set in his rest,
Into the thickest of death, through threat'ning peril prest,
To where he had perceiv'd the Earl in person drew,
Whose standard-bearer he sir William Brandon slew,
The pile of his strong staff into his arm-pit sent;
When, at a second shock, down Sir John Cheney went,
Which scarce a lance's length before the Earl was plac'd,
Untill by Richmond's guard environed at last,
With many a cruel wound was through the body gride.
Upon this fatal field John duke of Norfolk died;
The stout lord Ferrers fell, and Ratcliffe, that had long
Of Richard's counsels been, found in the field among
A thousand soldiers that on both sides were slain.
O Redmore! then it seem'd thy name was not in vain,
When with a thousand's blood the earth was colour'd red.
Whereas th' imperial crown was set on Henry's head,
Being found in Richard's tent as he it there did win:
The cruel Tyrant stript to the bare naked skin,
Behind an Herald truss'd, was back to Leicester sent,
From whence the day before he to the battle went."

In the house of Mr. Roberts at Sutton, in pulling down an old wainscot, there was discovered a large quantity of old writings, which were found to contain an account of the battle of Bosworth Field*; but, as no particular notice was then taken of the MSS. or value set upon them, they were all actually destroyed by the cook

---

* I preserve this anecdote as the tradition of the neighbourhood, without giving much credit to the importance of the MSS. supposed to have been destroyed; which possibly might have been a copy from some of the old Chroniclers, or perhaps only some common black-letter book. The tradition, however, was thus confirmed to me, in 1793, by the following letter from a friend at Bosworth: "Mrs. Jane Dixie has many times stated, that she could remember reading in the papers alluded to; and that she recollected something about the King stopping at the Well; and about his natural son

for culinary purposes. It is said there were four or five quires of them.

On the 17th of June, 1789, I had the satisfaction of traversing this important scene; and the result of the observations then made was thus communicated to one of my companions in the excursion:

"To DAVID WELLS, of Burbach, Esq. F.S.A.

Dear Sir – By the united ingenuity of our good friends Mr. Robinson and Mr. Pridden, I have obtained, what you and I have long been wishing for, a plan of the memorable spot where Richard's career of empire was concluded with loss of life.

"With much pleasure do I reflect on the excursion which gave birth to this inquiry. The variety of adventures experienced in the course of a single day recurs in full force to recollection. The transitions of weather, from the calmness of the morning at our leaving Hinckley, to the excessive violence of a thunder-storm in Sutton Field; the comfort we experienced, whilst the storm raged terribly around, in the shelter afforded by *Bickley's* deserted cottage*; the hospitable roof of the benevolent farmer at Shenton;

being placed on such a hill, and of the king being set fast in a bog; how another man gave him his horse, and the king mounted a second time; likewise the king cleaving Sir William Brandon the Earl's standard-bearer down the head at one blow. She mentioned, that she read of Henry being quite in the rear (who seemed a coward to the King); and that the King, being on the hill with his Son, declared he was betrayed, but that he would die a hero, or wash his hands in Henry's blood, &c. I have heard her talk of it several times, and she had a great deal to say about it: she thought it the only true copy. About the year 1750, several pieces of money were found by bricklayers in various places, supposed to have been hidden at the time of the Battle. I saw several of the pieces; but what kind of coin they were, I don't remember; there were about 150 of them, hid in different places about Sutton and Bosworth."

* "It was during the inevitable confinement under this cottage, marked B. in the Plan, that we were entertained and edified by your conversation with Mr. Robinson on Electricity. It was here also that our friends took a considerable part of the observations which have furnished the Map; and here the Writer of this Letter amused himself by penning the hasty Sonnet which you was so partial as to commend, though it had no other merit than locality of situation, as you will readily confess on seeing it in print:

the unexpected magnificence of his truly noble mansion*; the splendour of a state-room adorned with inter-marriages recorded by ornamental blazonry, though now used only as a granary; the keen appetites we carried to our dinner (from the late hour I should rather say *supper*) at the comfortable inn at Market Bosworth; and the accidents which our good friend Robinson so narrowly escaped from the impetuosity of his *high-mettled steed*; the long, but not unpleasant, walk which closed the tranquil evening (an evening which was marked in the Metropolis by terror and confusion†); are all as fresh in memory as an event of yesterday.

"It was the precise season, let me observe, when the blossom of the hawthorn, assuming its deepest vermeil tincture, was on the point of expanding into bud; when the red and the white rose full-blown (apt emblems of the scenery we contemplated) were literally entwined in beauteous embrace; and the flaunting woodbine, thrusting forth in luxuriant stem, began to exhibit delicious fragrance. To an astonished traveller, who had long been 'pent in populous city,' the very hedges were a garden; the meadows and

> 'Sutton, thy friendly cottage let me hail,
> Whilst, shelter'd from the tempest's furious yell,
> We calmly view the memorable vale
> Where England's bold Usurper bravely fell.
> Still strongly mark'd th'ensanguin'd plain appears,
> Where clos'd, fierce Richard, thy untimely fate;
> And Stoke's proud fane its lofty spire uprears,
> Where Henry first assum'd the Kingly State.
> Thy Cemeteries, Dadlington, declare
> The dreadful carnage of th'embattled train:
> And Ambiem's leafy groves will ever bear
> The sombre vestige of the Heroes slain.
> Oh, may henceforth domestic tumult cease,
> And England's sons enjoy perpetual peace!'

* A view of Shenton Hall, which was then inhabited by one of the tenants, is here given. The house has since been considerably improved, and is now a handsome mansion, the residence of Colonel Wollaston, the worthy owner of the lordship. The Coats of Arms are in the Hall and Chapel.

† The Opera-house in the Haymarket was consumed that evening by fire.

SHENTON HALL.

J. Prudden. del. June 17 1789.

T. Bannerman Sculp.

richly-cultivated fields a paradise. Could a more exquisite point of time have been selected? I see at this moment the waving corn through which we walked to Sutton church, so neatly delineated in Mr. Pridden's landscape*; the mantling ivy on the mouldering gateway of the hall-house†, once the residence of the respectable family of *Roberts*; the curious devices, particularly the well-adapted roses, embossed on the walls of the building now hastening to sad decay; and the pleasing monument of sir William's benevolence in the charitable foundation established by him in the village.

"Determining to make it a day of philosophical and antiquarian research, our first stage from Hinckley was only a single mile along the Derby road; where the Gravel-pit, so productive of curious Fossils, arrested our attention, and well deserved it. On these wonderful productions I shall not here enlarge; as your cabinet and Mr. Robinson's have already furnished the publick with a beautiful plate§.

"The celebrated *Spreading Elm*, in the lane leading from the Gravel-pit to Barwell, which preserved the life of Captain Shenton during the civil wars in a manner somewhat similar to the Royal Oak of his Sovereign, I shall also barely mention, as Mr. Robinson has already given both a drawing and a particular description of it‡.

"Two miles further we reached Stapleton, where Richard encamped the night before his fatal battle; a village now remarkable

---

* See a view of it in the History of Leicestershire, vol. IV. pl. LXXXVII. p. 544.

† See also a view of this old Gateway (since demolished) in the same volume, plate LXXXVII. p. 544.

§ See the History of Leicestershire, vol. IV. Plate LXXXIII. p. 462; and the Natural History of the Vale of Belvoir, in the First Volume, p. cxci.

‡ "This tree, which is a wich-elm, sends out large arms, or branches, about seven or eight feet from the ground, and the lower part of it is remarkably thick: the upper part looks much younger. – This venerable old tree many look upon as a kind of prodigy. As to the natural cause, it is evident to the diligent observer, that a vast quantity of flies are produced in the leaves of the elm and many other trees. We are very sensible of this in our gardens, by the curling up of the leaves of choice fruit-trees, especially when clammy mildews, &c. assist in the production of these insects; for on the under-side of the leaves, where the eggs and spawn are deposited, the envenom'd leaf swells into a kind of blister, and forms a kind of concavity for their

Throsby pinx.ᵗ

RICHMOND's Army advancing on

W&J Walker sculp.

the eve of Battle to meet **RICHARD's**.

for little more than its plain unornamented church; and at the fourth mile on the turnpike-road an easy turn conveyed us to Sutton Cheynell, where we were to enter on the business of tracing out, from actual observation, in conjunction with our accurate companions, the precise situation of the two Armies, both before and at the time of their engagement; a task that was the less difficult as both Mr. Robinson and Mr. Hutton had already taken much laudable pains to investigate this curious desideratum in English History.

"Our horses, you well remember, were left at Sutton; concluding that on foot we should be better able to explore

> 'each lane, and every alley green,
> Dingle, or bushy dell of the wild wood,
> And every bosky bourn from side to side.'

"Our guide was Mr. Robinson*; who, on the precise 300th anniversary from the day on which the battle was fought, had traversed the ground; and has given his opinion in so concise a way, that I cannot do better than transcribe his words: 'I have often,' he says, 'been on the spot. The few trees I have drawn represent the *Ambiem* wood, which is but small. On the side next Hinckley is some tender ground, where it is said the King's horse was mired; and on the other side of the wood is King Richard's Well. The *Ambiem* is supposed to be the place of the engagement; but there are many opinions of the position of the line of battle, which the following, I think, will sufficiently determine. Richmond is said to have taken a particular position for securing his right wing, &c.; and by so doing, it is agreed, he had the sun on his

---

security, and at the same time yields a kind of ichor or humidity for their support. That this has been the case with the tree in question I doubt not, from the great number of small branches, and the protuberances on the large arms in the lower part of the tree. This tree is, however, well worthy of notice; and, I think, we may compute its age at about 174 years at least; viz. about 40 years when sufficient for a hiding-place, to which if we add 134 years since the Battle of Worcester, the sum will be 174. The girth in the middle of the butt is five feet 10 inches." J.R. – See a view of this remarkable Tree in the Fourth Volume of the History of Leicestershire, vol. IV. pl. LXXVI. p. 477.

* See a Portrait and some Memoirs of Mr. Robinson in the History of Leicestershire, vol. IV. Pl. CXVIII. p. 693.

back, and full in the face of his enemies; and the battle is recorded to have been fought on the 22d of August, 1485, at two o'clock in the afternoon. If, therefore, we draw a meridian on the spot, and another line to the Westward of the same, making an angle of 30°, and then intersect the same at right angles, we have the position of the line of battle as drawn in my Map. The King's army, consisting of 16,000, would make an extensive line; and that of Richmond being hardly one-third of the number, it would be necessary to secure his wings in the best manner possible; therefore, it is said, he secured the right wing with a morass, and probably the left with the brook at Shenton, in which position he would have Dadlington brook in his rear.'

"Assisted by the ingenious ideas of Mr. Hutton, we again and again compared the local situation; and I have every reason to believe that the plan now given is tolerably exact; and to that I may venture to refer, as the clearest account of the spot that has ever yet been delineated*.

"With the repetition of historical facts, I shall not at present tire you†. If you are inclined to consult the Chronicles of the times, you may find them amply detailed in Holinshed, vol. II. p. 753; in Speed, p. 947-952; in the various particular Biographers of Richard the Third and Henry the Seventh; or in any of the more general Historians.

"I remain, dear Sir, yours faithfully,

"*March* 31, 1790.   J. NICHOLS.

"P.S.   I herewith add, in elucidation of the Plan [see pages 144 & 145] of the Battle of Bosworth, carefully surveyed in its several

---

* In the annexed Plate is given a conjectural View of the Battle, as delineated by Mr. Throsby.

† I had fondly hoped to have gratified a worthy friend by this recital of a day's adventure, in which he bore a considerable part; but "what," says Dr. Johnson, "are the hopes of man!" I am "disappointed by the stroke of Death!" So lately as the day on which the letter bears date, Mr. Wells saw it in MS. and was delighted with the idea of its being speedily to appear in print. Whilst the sheet which contained the letter was first actually passing through the press, I learnt, with inexpressible concern, that he died, of a putrid fever, on Saturday May 1, 1790. "His studies had been various, and his acquaintance with books was great." See his portrait, and a biographical account of him, in the History of Leicestershire, vol. IV. Plate LXIX. p. 460.

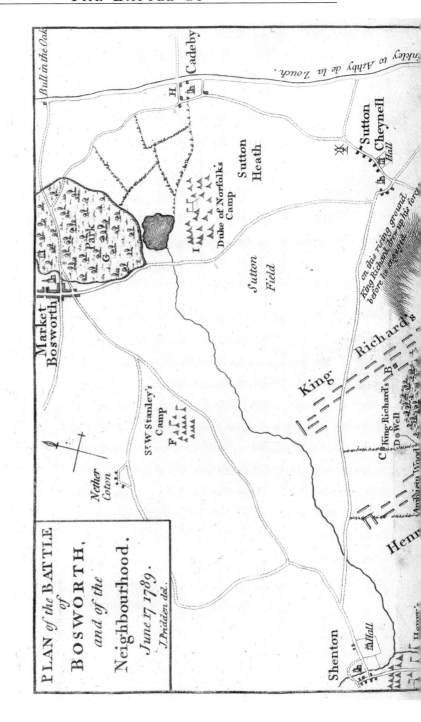

PLAN of the BATTLE
of
BOSWORTH,
and of the
Neighbourhood.
June 17 1789.
J.Pridden del.

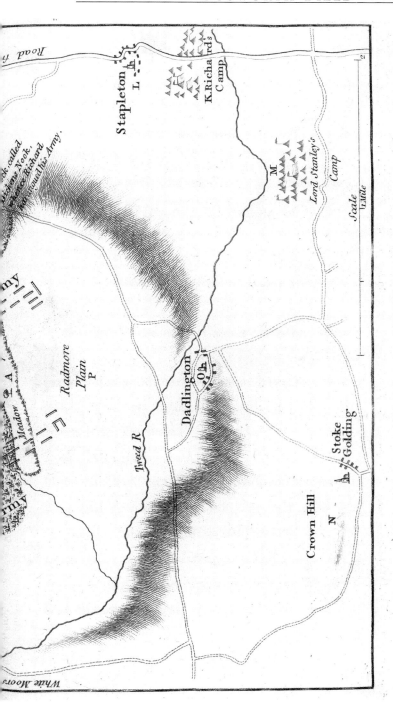

points by us all, and delineated by Mr. Pridden, the result of the remarks of various explorers of this interesting and historic portion of the County, and of our own inquiries and observations."

Key to the Map:

A. A small morass, or bog, near which it is said King Richard's horse was mired. Here is a small oak, and several shrubs growing upon it; the rest of the ground about it is tolerably dry.

B. A cottage, late Bickley's, now Morris's, uninhabited.

C. Hewitt's cottage, uninhabited.

D. A small spring, called *King Richard's Well*.

E. The White-moors, near Shenton, where Henry encamped the night before the battle. Hither John Herdwick, who lived at Lindley-hall, about three miles off, led the van down into the field.

F. Hanging-hill, near Nether Coton. Here Sir William Stanley pitched his camp. This hill is very steep on the side towards the field; and here he could observe the motions of the two Armies. Lord Stanley's camp being on the opposite hill, where he had the same advantage, they were enabled to act in conjunction, by signals from each other: this plan was pre-concerted in the interview with Henry at Atherston. Sir William Stanley halted at Temple-hall, a very high hill, where he threw up some breast-works, but found he was too far from the main Army.

G. Bosworth Park.

H. Cadeby. The Duke of Norfolk came through this village, on his way to the camp; and here he gained information how each army was situated.

I. Duke of Norfolk's camp. The site of this camp in 1485 was a wood, which joined the other. It was cut down in 1748; and is now converted into a farm. In stubbing up the roots, and clearing the ground, there were found various instruments of war; spears, swords, arrows, battle-axes (many of them very sharp-pointed), scull-caps, breast-plates, and above a dozen knives, one of which was about 12 inches long. Most of these curiosities are preserved, by Mr. Pochin, at Bosworth Hall.

K. Dicken's Nook; a hillock whence King Richard harangued his Army. Here the Duke of Norfolk joined the King. On the rising ground to the North-west King Richard drew up his forces before he engaged; and on an eminence near this station the King placed his natural son, to see the result of the day; who, if the battle should be lost, was to make off in disguise; which he accordingly did, and afterwards, it is said, learned the trade of a stone-mason.

L. Stapleton; where King Richard encamped the night before the battle.

L. Ambiem-wood.

M. Ambiem-hill. At the top of this hill was Lord Stanley's camp.

N. Crown-hill, near Stoke Golding. Henry pursued the King's forces to this place; and on it he was invested with the Royal Crown. It still retains the name of *Crown Hill*, or *King Harry's Hill*.

O. Dadlington. Indented spaces of ground, probably the graves of the victims in this bloody battle, are visible in several spots about this village.

P. Radmore-plain, commonly called *Sutton Cow-posture*, where the battle began; and where the two Stanleys, descending from the adjoining hills with their reserved forces, cut the communication off between the King and his main Army; and led to the decision of the business of this important day.

Sir *John Savage* junior, of Clifton, co. Chester (second earl Rivers), commanded the left wing at the battle in Bosworth field; for which Henry VII. gave him, *cum allis*, the manor of Shepeshed, &c. and the estates of sir Francis Lovell*.

Richard Boughton, sheriff for Warwickshire and Leicestershire, was killed in Bosworth field.

A Sacheverell, killed there, is buried in Morley church, near Derby.

William Gilpin was slain in Bosworth Field†.

An act of attainder was passed in Parliament with all possible expedition, which begins thus: "Forasmoche as every King, Prince, and Liege Lord, the more hie that he be in estate and prehemenence, the more singularly he is bound to the advancement and preferring of that indefferent vertue Justice; and promoteinge and rewardinge Vertue and bi oppressinge and punishinge Vice: Wherefore oure Soveraigne Lord, calleinge unto hys blessed remembraunce thys high and grete charge adjoyned to hys Royall Majestie and Estate, not oblivious nor puttinge out of hys godly mind the unnaturall, mischeivous, and grete perjuries, treasons, homicides, and murdres, in shedding of infants blood, with manie other wronges, odious offences, and abominac'ons ayenst God

---

* Sir Peter Leycester, p. 232.

† Hutchinson's History of Durham, vol. II. p. 349.

and man, and in esp'all oure said Soveraigne Lord, committed and doone by Richard late Duke of Glouc', callinge and nameinge hymself, by usurpac'on, King Richard the III[d]; the which, with John late duke of Norff', Thomas erle of Surrie, Francis Lovell kn't visc' Lovell, Walter devereux kn't, late lord Ferrers, John lord Zouche, Robert Harrington, Richard Charleton, Richard Ratcliffe, William Berkeley of Welley, Robert Brakenbury, Thomas Pilkinton, Robert Midletoune, James Harrington, kn'ts; Walter Hopton, William Catesby, Roger Wake, William Sapcott, Humfrey Stafford, William Clerke of Wenlocke, Jeffrey S't Jermin, Richard Watkins, herrauld of armes, Richard Revell of Derbishyre, Thomas Poulter of the countee of Kent the younger, John Walsh otherwyse called Hastinges, John Kendale, late secretarie to the said Richard late duke, John Buck, Andrew Ratt, and William Branton of Burford, the xxI[st] daie of August, the first yere of the reign of oure Soveraigne Lord, assembled to theyme atte Leicestre in the countee of Leycestre a grete hoste, traiterously intendinge, imagininge, and conspireinge, the destrucc'on of the Kinges royall p'soune, oure Soveraigne Leige lord. And they, with the same hoste, with banners spred, mightyly armed and defenced with all manner armes, as gunnes, bowes, arrowes, speres, gleves, axes, and all other manner articles apt or needfull to gef and cause mightie battaille agen oure said Soveraine Lord, kept togedre from the said xxII[d] daie of the said month thanne next followinge, and theyme conduced to a feld within the said shyre of Leicestre, there bi grete and continued deliberac'one, traiterously levied warre ayenst oure said Soverayne Lord, and his true subjects there being in his service and assistance under a banner of oure said Soveraine Lord, to the subversion of this realme, and com'on weale of the same*."

By this Act, the above persons are all declared traitors, and their estates forfeited; with an exeption in favour of John Catesbie, knight, Thomas Kennel, and William Ashby, esquires, for the manor of Kirbie-upon-Wretheck, in the county of Leicester, and of other lands and tenements in Kirbie, Stretton, Somerby, Thorp Segfeld, and Godebie, which they had of the gift and feoffment of Thomas Davis and John Bye†.

* Rot. Parl. 1 Hen. VII. vol. VI. p. 276.

† Ibid. 277.

"A co'mission to all officers, ffermors, tenents, and other occupyers of the lordship of Market Bosworth, to accept sir Marmaduke Constable as owner of ye said lordships, and to content unto him all there rents and duties of there fermes and tenures, from Michaelmas last past, and so for thensforth; and to ayde him in entring into the said lordships. Yeven the xxviii day of March, a° primo*."

The death of Richard, and subsequent conduct of Henry, are thus related by Charles Aleyan†.

> "He like a Bore (his bearing was the Bore*,
> A cognisance which with his minde agrees)
> Broke up the rankes to Richmond's selfe, and tore
> Men up like trees; men that are like to trees
> Inverst; but Richmond he extirped not.
> 'Non tibi spiro,' was this Rose's mott.
>
> There an untutour'd fortitude did try
> Experimentall valour, personall strength;
> That is, soft Richmond Richard did defie,
> And warded the Bore's tuskes at his sworde's length:
> You could not have a cleaner valour seene,
> Though Magnaminity had incarnate beene.
>
> And his impression in his souldiers' hearts
> Made them his medals; he like chymicke fire
> Put soules of gold into their earthy parts;
> And by his mountures taught them to aspire:
> Actions of Kings are precepts; what they doe
> Seeme to be precedents, and warrants too.
>
> Exempli gratia's teach not; but compell;
> There's no such Canon as Authoritie;
> They do their doctrine tacitly refell,
> Who with their acts doe not exemplifie:
> Men practise what they see by Leaders done;
> Not Cæsar's Ito, but his Veni won.

---

* Harl. MSS. 433. p. 168. a.

† In his "History of Henry the Seventh."

§ See the seal in the Plate, fig. 9, p. 157.

Now Conquest with her wings fan'd every side
With equall hope, and strooke with equall feare:
Like scales with constant motion they slide,
Now that is upward, and now this is there:
And Henrie's faith with feares, yet hopes was mix'd,
Like to those starres which tremble, yet are fix'd.

The Ancients gave a spheare to Victory,
On which her feete stand giddie and uneven;
But hence just causes draw alacrity,
Her hands are holden by the hand of Heaven:
Here's Henrie's feare, she on a spheare doth stand;
Here's Henrie's hope, Jove holds her by the hand.

As thus the question doubtfully did stand,
And unconcluded; Stanly did come on
With sword, and a decision in his hand:
Thus under the equator, when the Sunne
With hottest flames tosteth the people's skinne,
The constant breeze brings a coole rescue in.

The case at worst Stanley determines it,
The souldiers' cries this martiall court adjourne;
And temper Danger in her highest fit,
were Daphne woman still, she'd sooner turne
A Laurell to crowne him, than to escape
The lustfull charges of Apollo's rape.

Yet Richard with such rage himselfe commits
With the whole hoast, that he may make the story
Question'd 'though writ by Truth: but these strong fits
Were lightnings before death; for this world's glory
Is figur'd in the Moone, they both waxe dull,
And suffer their eclipses in their full.

And now I see him sinke: his eyes did make
A shot like falling starres: flash out, and done:
Groaning he did a stately farewell take,
And in his night of death set like the Sunne;
For Richard in his West seem'd greater, than
When Richard shin'd in his Meridian.

Three years he acted ill, these two houres well,
And with unmated resolution strove:
He fought as bravely, as he justly fell.
As did the Capitoll to Manlius prove,
So Bosworth did to him, the monument
Both of his glory and his punishment.

Here leave his dust incorporate with mould;
He was a King; that challengeth respect:
Passe by his tombe in silence, as of old
They did their heroes temples, and erect
An Altar to Oblivion, while I
Another build to Henrie's memory.

This fortune swel'd not Henry to a brave;
Mercy step'd in, and brought a prohibition:
Those are best temper'd fortitudes which have
Some graines of pittie in their composition:
Valour's the iron virtue; yet abates
Nought of herselfe with silke upon her plates.

The wreath of conquest in a generous minde
Is an inducement to a moderation;
In all exalted spirits you shall finde
Something of humblenesse for mitigation:
And Old Rome built, as Marius thought best,
The Fane of Honour lower than the rest.

He conquer'd, yet ay prostrate in the field
(His sacred campe did like a temple looke):
Where Henry first did stand, noe Henry kneel'd,
And chang'd his sword into a prayer-booke;
And solemnely did a Te Deum say;
Heaven's a kinde Creditour, whom thanks can pay.

Care and his Crowne met at his head together;
He is no sooner king, but he must be
An Œdipus, and solve his riddle, whether
He'le claime by wife, or birth, or victory:
But for this triple knot, Henry had stor'd
A triple wedge, and broke this threefold cord.

If by his wife, he in effect had sayd
The line of Yorke was better than his owne:
Or why should man, who is the woman's head,
To a woman's hand doe homage for a crowne?
And Henry thought it an unkingly thing,
To have his crowne indebted to his ring.

Nor would he claime by conquest, or give part
Unto the sword: for that would but affright
The Realme to forc'd obedience, and start
Men into giddy subjects; for it might
Make their faith stagger, and obedience reele,
If Henrie's scepter had beene made of steele.

At last his love to himselfe made the case plaine,
That titles royall in his blood did flow,
And every veine was a basilick veine:
This made him absolute: Henry did know,
That Princes were most independent when
Their crowne to hold of Nature, not of men.

Having thus defin'd, which sodainely was done,
(For's consultation and his choyse did goe
Together,) in a progresse he set on
For London, in a coach* unseene, and so
Appearing not, some God appear'd to be,
Whom men adore, and yet no shape doe see.

Then orisons and humnes at Paule's were sung,
And (as before) Te Deum sung agen;
His banners in the church for off'rings hung.
When Henry pray'd in th' armie, the campe then
Appear'd a church; when he his banners rear'd
Within the church, the church a camp appear'd.

Suspicion now whisper'd these aires about,
That Henry was not reall: every head
That could not cleare, yet could create this doubt,
That Henry never would with England wed,
And joyne with Yorke: how can a sheete enfold
Two Houses, which a Kingdom could not hold?

This doubt had ground; for he had given some hope
To match with Brettaigne: but his case requir'd
Some reservation, and another scope
Than he pretended, or than they desir'd:
In common tracts great actions must not goe,
Here that's the King's highway, which fewest know.

To hush this talke, he promis'd faithfully
To match at home; and make this noise appeare
A fable, gotten in adultery,
Betweene a scandalous tongue and itching eare:
Bad them trust Henry, not the buzze of Fame,
Which, like some hound, opens where is no game.

* One should like to see the picture of it. Richard II. rode through London in a whirlicote. Stow. – Grammont has told us that the first glass-coach appeared in Charles the Second's time. G. ASHBY

His Coronation then he hastened
Which (that the title might be all his owne)
Before the marriage was accomplished,
Least she might seeme a sharer in the crowne:
For, though in other loves 'tis strange, yet he
Knew that his love might here his rivall be.

And for his glory and his safety too,
He did erect the guard. Henry conjoin'd
Things different in themselves – what none could doe –
The two discordant roses he combin'd:
And, which have rarely beene allied by Fate,
He did unite security and state.

Then call'd a Parliament, so to proclaime
That Justice was the rule he'de governe by;
And that a crowne alone was not his ayme;
Thus Hercules, constelled in the skie,
Though with one hand he at the Crowne doth reach,
He doth the other to the Balance stretch.

There with a generall pardon he allaies
The feares of th' adverse party: he did finde
That feares lodg'd in a subject's brest can raise
A dangerous passion: as we see combin'd
Th' order of causes in the chaine of Fate,
So 'tis in passions; if we feare, we hate."

The Battle of Bosworth, enameled on a jewel usually worn by King Henry VIII. was sold among King Charles the First's pictures; and is said by Sir Joseph Ayloffe, in 1770, to have been then in the possession of the Hon. Horace Walpole*.

Mr. Burton mentions many curiosities having been found; of which several are yet preserved. A pair of gilt spurs, found on the site of the Field of Battle, are kept with great care in the church-chest at Bosworth.

In the very curious and extensive Museum of my late friend Mr. Richard Greene, of Lichfield, was "An amulet, or charm, being a ring of brass found on the Field of Battle near Bosworth."

In the same very curious cabinet was the very elegant Cross-bow, found also in Bosworth Field, and delineated in the annexed Plate [pages 155-157], fig. 1. *a. b.* In the same Plate, fig. 2. and 3. are spear-heads, of which, as well as of arrows, great numbers have been found.

---

* Archæologia, vol. III, p. 190. But I have Lord Orford's express authority, in a letter to myself, by his immediate direction, for saying that it was not there. J.N.

Fig. 4. is a sword, with a very strong iron guard, or basket, sufficient to repel a severe blow from an enemy. The outer part of the hilt is gone; the blade is long and narrow, and has only one edge, except towards the point; the whole length, from the pommel to the point, is four feet. This sword had been in possession of the Darker family many years; and came, through the hands of Mr. Wheatley of Hinckley (who bought it at the sale of the effects of Mr. Darker of Barwell) to the well-stored Museum of Mr. Richard Fowke of Elmsthorpe.

Two other swords, fig. 5. and 6. are preserved, by Mr. Perkins, at Orton-on-the-Hill; amd Mr. Babington, at Rothley Temple. Fig. 7. *a.* and *b.* are in the extensive Museum at Liverpool. A brass thumb-ring, found in the field where the battle was fought, impressed with the moon and seven stars, and now in my possession, is engraved in fig. 8.

A gold seal-ring*, fig. 9, on which was enameled a white boar, fell into the hands of the late Dr. Charles Mason, of Trinity College, Cambridge; after whose death, it was bought for William the fifth Duke of Devonshire, and thus illustrated by Dr. Pegge, in a letter to Dr. Lort:

"The Duke of Devonshire's seal-ring, of which, by his Grace's favour, I have an impression, is a very fine jewel. It weights nearly 12 dwts. and is in the best and highest preservation, being perfect, as I remember, in every respect. The inscription over the boar is, *S. th: Enche*, or *Euche*. That is, when written at length, Sigillum *Thomæ Euche*, for so I would read it rather than *Enche*, and my reason will obviously appear below.

"The French motto in the inside of the orbicle of the ring is, *Honeur & joye*. To bestow a few words on the subject: This, Sir, is the only example I have ever seen of an inscription placed in a seal-ring in the area of the gem along with the device; the legends being commonly written in a circle round the stone, and not cut upon it as here.

"As I find no English family of the name of *Enche* or *Euche* in my books, nor at the Heralds' Office, which I have consulted for the

---

* "I was always disposed to think this seal belonged to one of Richard the Third's followers; and that the boar was his badge or cognizance; and the motto his too, Fraunche, Frank; Free, liberal; and that Shakespeare alluded to it in a very perverted sense: 'My son George Stanley hath he franked in hold;' from boars being fed freely, though confined: but the S prefixed makes me doubt. Q. Stephen, or Simon, Fr.? Usually it would stand for Sigillum; but then, I think, a Christian name would follow." G. ASHBY.

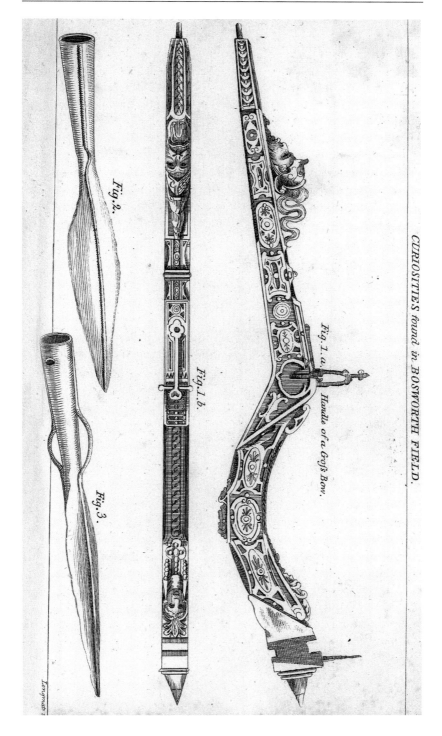

CURIOSITIES found in BOSWORTH FIELD.

Fig. 1. a. Handle of a Cross Bow.

Fig. 1. b.

Fig. 2.

Fig. 3.

Longman's

CURIOSITIES found in BOSWORTH FIELD.

Fig. 4

3 feet 3 inches.

Fig. 5

Fig. 7. a.

Fig. 6.

Fig. 7. b.

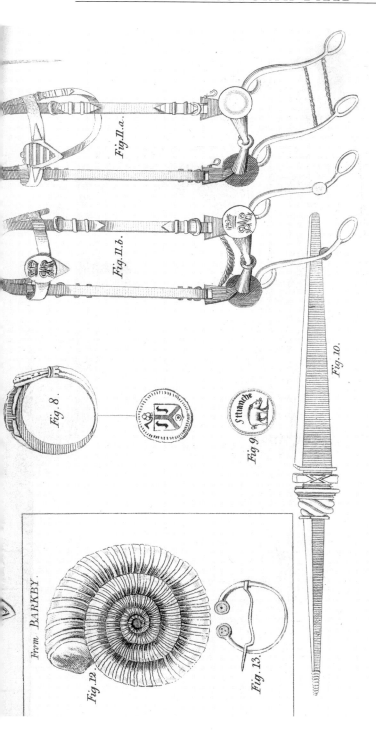

Fig.II.a.

Fig.II.b.

Fig.10.

Fig.8.

Fig.9.

S.tranghe

From BARKBY.

Fig.12.

Fig.13.

purpose, I incline to think that *Euche*, pronounced *Euke*, is a British or Welsh name. *Hŵch*, in that language, is a hog or a boar, and our English word *hog* is borrowed from it. I need to observe to you, Sir, that the Heralds, in assigning both their bearings and cognizances, very frequently allude to the sound or meaning of the person's name; just as here they appear to have given the device of a boar or hog, *Hŵch* in British, to a person of the name of *Euke*. I have known people of the names of Pig, Boar, and Hog, in England, just as we have in Latin *Aper, Verres, Scrofa*, &c.*; and why not Euke or Hŵch among the Britons? It certainly is not the name of a place, whence many of our surnames are taken, because it wants the necessary prefix *de*. Many, no doubt, will recollect the story of *Arrius Aper*, upon this occasion; but, as every body may not, I will briefly report it: *Aper* was father-in-law to the promising young emperor Numerianus†, and his murderer; but was immediately seized, and laid in prison. Diocletian succeeded Numerianus; and he, when a private man, had been told by a Druidess, that he should *obtain the empire when he had killed a boar*. After he was proclaimed emperor by the soldiers, he caused *Aper* to be brought to him, reproached him with the murder of his prince, and then, coming down from the tribunal whence he had been speaking, he stabbed him himself, and observed upon him, 'that he had killed the fatal boar.' And the Historian observes, he would never had begun his reign with an act of cruelty, had he not had in his eye the Druidical prediction above-mentioned, and been desirous of fulfilling it. This, Sir, you must allow, is exceedingly *àpropos,* since there is an allusion in the creature or animal to the name, in the very same manner as the device on the ring points, according to our interpretation, to the name of the owner.

"To return, Henry VII. landed in Wales, when he came to England, and upon his expedition against Richard III.; and he had many Britons, particularly gentlemen, in his army. *Euche* was probably one of them, as he seems to have been a person of note: and therefore, though the white boar was the badge of Richard, and though, considering the place where the ring was found, *viz.*

---

* Carr. Sigon. de Nom. Rom. p. 356, 358, 359, 360.

† Veniscus, Numerian. p. 302.

in Bosworth Field, some people may be led to imagine Thomas Euke might be a retainer of his, escially as it was common for dependants to take the arms, or crests, or badges, of their patrons, with the proper variations, yet this ring may much more reasonable be thought, upon the ground of history, to belong to one of Henry's party than to one of Richard's. SAM. PEGGE."

Fig. 10. is one of the knives found in the Duke of Norfolk's Camp*. Fig. 11. is an old bridle found on the site of the Field of Battle, but not likely to be so antient as the time of Richard. Fig. 12. 13. are a Cornu Ammonis, and a Fibula, found at Barkby; aand communicated by the Rev. Henry Woodcock.

At the distance of 160 years, Bosworth Field again became the theatre of war; as appears by the following letter, which was published in 1644 by Parliamentary authority†.

"Worthy Sir – This day's success, so far beyond expectation, hath hastened these lines, as I promised, to give you a speedy account of our proceedings here. This morning intelligence was brought to our horse-quarters that the enemy were plundering about Hinckley; whereupon my noble Lord Gray, being ever ready of any opportunity to serve his country, forthwith sent out a well-resolved party, under the command of Captain Babington, consisting of 80 good horse. They marched towards Bosworth Field, where they overtook 120 of Hastings's forces, and there fought with them, in the very place where King Richard was slain. At the first charge, the enemy fled; our men made a hot pursuit for three miles, killed six, wounded many, took 40 prisoners, a list whereof I have inclosed, as truly collected as the short time will permit; for I believe, upon further examination, there will be found a greater number of officers there are here named; for the habits and postures of

---

* See before, p. 146.

† Extracted from "A Copy of a Letter sent from the Lord Fairfax to the Mayor of Hull; and by him sent to the Committee of both Kingdoms; concerning the great Victory obtained against Prince Rupert about the Raising the Siege at York. Also a true Relation of a defeat given to Colonel Hastings by the Lord Gray's Forces, July 1, 1644, at Bosworth Field, in the very place where King Richard the Third was slain: With the Names of such Commanders and Soldiers as were slain and taken. Printed, according to Order, July 6, 1644."

many of the prisoners give just cause to suspect their condition to be far above common Troopers. We lost not one man; Captain Babington shot in the hand, whose behaviour I cannot pass: At the discovery of the Enemy, he made a stand, and gave strict command to his soldiers to forbear plunder, but to go on courageously with him; and promised them, on the word of a Gentleman, that if the day proved theirs (which he feared not, with God's assistance), what prize should be gained from the Enemy should be theirs. This succeeded, and is performed accordingly. There was also wounded on our party the Quarter-master to Sir Edward Hartopp; he is shot in the thigh, and a common soldier or two slightly wounded. And, to make our success the greater this was done after we had three days hard march, and but four hours refreshment before this design was undertaken (our forces being called back from their march to sir William Waller, upon intelligence of the enemy's design to plunder our country.) We attribute all to the Giver of Victories.

"I pray you let us hear what good news the West affords; which will be as welcome to us, as I am confident this will be to you. If you intend correspondency, be as diligent to take opportunity as is,

"Your most affectionate friend and servant,

"FAIRFAX.,

"*Leicester, July* 1, 1644.

"My Lord is now gone out in person, in pursuit of Colonel Nevill and colonel Pate, who are plundering the other` side of the country. We pray for his good success.

"Three-score horses taken. One hundred cattle, besides sheep and other goods in a very great proportion, rescued and restored to the owners."